MW01167086

Futuring Tools for Strategic Quality Planning in Education

Also Available from ASQ Quality Press

Improving Student Learning: Applying Deming's Quality Principles in Classrooms
Lee Jenkins

Quality Team Learning for Schools: A Principal's Perspective
James E. Abbott

Orchestrating Learning With Quality
David P. Langford and Barbara A. Cleary, Ph.D.

Kidgets: And Other Insightful Stories About Quality In Education
Maury Cotter and Daniel Seymour

Tools and Techniques to Inspire Classroom Learning
Barbara A. Cleary and Sally J. Duncan

The Quality Toolbox
Nancy R. Tague

Mapping Work Processes
Dianne Galloway

Team Fitness
Meg Hartzler and Jane E. Henry, Ph.D.

The Change Agents' Handbook: A Survival Guide for Quality Improvement Champions
David W. Hutton

Quality Quotes
Hélio Gomes

To request a complimentary catalog of ASQ Quality Press publications, call 800-248-1946.

Futuring Tools for Strategic Quality Planning in Education

by

Dr. William F. Alexander
The College of New Jersey

and

Dr. Richard W. Serfass
Quality New Jersey

ASQ Quality Press
Milwaukee, Wisconsin

Futuring Tools for Strategic Quality Planning in Education
William F. Alexander and Richard W. Serfass

Library of Congress Cataloging-in-Publication Data

Alexander, William F.
    Futuring tools for strategic quality planning in education / by
  William F. Alexander and Richard W. Serfass.
        p.   cm.
    Includes bibliographic references (p.).
    ISBN 0-87389-442-1
    1. Educational planning—United States.   2. School
  management and organization—United States.   3. Strategic
  planning—United States.   4. Organizational change—United
  States.   I. Serfass, Richard W.   II. Title.
  LC89.A58   1998
  371.2'07'0973—dc21   98-37412
                                                CIP

© 1999 by ASQ

10 9 8 7 6 5 4 3

ISBN 0-87389-442-1
Acquisitions Editor: Ken Zielske
Project Editor: Annemieke Koudstaal
Production Coordinator: Shawn Dohogne

ASQ Mission: The American Society for Quality advances individual and organizational performance excellence worldwide by providing opportunities for learning, quality improvement, and knowledge exchange.

Attention: Bookstores, Wholesalers, Schools and Corporations: ASQ Quality Press books, videotapes, audiotapes, and software are available at quantity discounts with bulk purchases for business, educational, or instructional use. For information, please contact ASQ Quality Press at 800-248-1946, or write to ASQ Quality Press, P.O. Box 3005, Milwaukee, WI 53201-3005.

To place orders or to request a free copy of the ASQ Quality Press Publications Catalog, including ASQ membership information, call 800-248-1946. Visit our web site at http://www.asq.org.
Printed in the United States of America

 Printed on acid-free paper

American Society for Quality

Quality Press
611 East Wisconsin Avenue
Milwaukee, Wisconsin 53202
Call toll free 800-248-1946
http://www.asq.org
http://standardsgroup.asq.org

Contents

Preface

Over the past few decades, our society has changed rapidly and dramatically. Planning for the future, while never easy, has become a formidable task for educational organizations. What was once expected to occur five to ten years in the future happens more immediately and abruptly. Whether dealing with changes in educational practice, increasing opportunities for technological applications, the societal implications of multiculturalism, funding issues, or the wars on poverty, drugs, illiteracy, and crime, educational leaders must now plan in a way that was not required of them in the past. The destiny of education is at stake and attention must be turned to long-range strategic planning with a clear direction for the future. *Strategic quality planning* focuses on this need and provides a higher level of scientific planning than is currently used. It requires organizations to establish their mission, vision, shared values, goals, and a procedure for the deployment of these goals throughout the organization.

The first of W. Edwards Deming's fourteen points for organizational transformation advises us to create constancy of purpose toward improvement of product or service. This point challenges us to establish a vision and work toward achieving that vision through continuous improvement. Vision is our window to the future.

Visions come in several varieties, many of which aspire to "best in class" or "world class status," and they present a list of objectives that is ambitious and hopeful. A vision is a dream of a possible future that sets a direction for an organization. It reflects the trailblazing efforts of an organization.

Visions are developed in a variety of ways ranging from brainstorming to use of sophisticated forecasting tools. The successful implementation of a vision is not guaranteed. A vision usually describes the *preferred* status of the organization in a specified future time period. However, planning teams must be aware that their future dream may be only *probable*, or worse, merely *possible*. This tiered concept of vision presents a need for organizations to examine their statements critically to determine what is forecast for the future and what to do about it.

Organizational visions often lack the systemic quality that gives them validity. It is not uncommon for a vision statement to be drafted during a committee meeting or short retreat where participants brainstorm ideas based upon their "perceptions du jour." Such procedures, however, lack the rigor of research and data collection on internal and external forces that are likely to have a significant impact on the vision points. Another weakness of visions is that they are often brief statements that are difficult to analyze for specific elements from which goals may be determined and assessments made.

A strategic quality future looks beyond vision. It incorporates the principles and techniques used in strategic planning and the quality improvement philosophy to produce a data-driven forecast that has high validity and a high probability of occurring. A strategic quality future overlays a systematic process on visioning. It tells us what we should be doing and when we should be doing it. It is a systematic approach to forecasting that employs research, discussion, assessment, analysis, and consensus to approximate, with a high degree of confidence, what the organization will be doing in the future time zone selected.

This scientific quality is obtained by filtering a vision through several analytical processes. One of these is *environmental scanning*, in which intense examinations of internal strengths and weaknesses, as well as external threats and opportunities, are conducted. Another is analysis of the *interrelationships of forecasted future events* with specific focus on their timing, positive or negative influence, and the magnitude of the influences on each other. *Benchmarking and vision sharing* of best-in-class organizations provide a valuable source of information on what works and what does not. Benchmarking and vision sharing among similar organizations provide a collaborative approach with a broad range of experience and high proba- bility for forecasting the future.

Tactical considerations are the result of those proactive decisions and actions that align organizational resources to work toward achievement of future goals. Aggressively developing market readiness, identifying new tar- get markets, monitoring competitors, and continuously assessing and improving services are tactical and drive the organization toward its strate- gic quality future. Educational leaders must now think tactically as well as operationally to lead their organizations into the future.

In the book *Competing for the Future*, Hamel and Prahalad (1994) remind us that the purpose is not to predict the future, but to imagine pos- sible futures. They call this "strategic architecture." The exhortation is to consider possible futures that regenerate the organization. The authors advise that organizational futures must reach beyond restructuring and reengineering to regeneration. This places high importance on the process used for developing vision, or beyond that, a strategic quality future.

Futuring Tools for Strategic Quality Planning in Education provides a set of practical tools that may be used by educators to accomplish the delicate yet complex task of future planning. Whether it be strategic planning or long- term or short-term planning, educational leaders must acquire an under- standing of tools and techniques that can assist them in creating a future for their organizations.

This book provides the reader with an understanding of the need for and the power of forecasting an organization's strategic future. More impor- tantly, it presents a set of futuring tools to enable leaders in education to plan for the future more effectively. The authors offer the following goals to accomplish this:

1. To develop an understanding of the terminology, timelines, and types of planning used in creating and developing the strategic quality future of an organization.

2. To understand the role of continuous improvement as the organi- zation develops plans to close the gap between where it is and where it wants to be.

3. To understand the process of strategic quality planning and its role in developing an organization's future.

4. To explain and give examples of futuring tools and how they are used to develop an organization's strategic future.

Futuring Tools for Strategic Quality Planning in Education also presumes that the environment of the organization is conducive to the philosophy prevalent in the quality movement. The writings in the current literature use terms such as *total quality management, continuous quality improvement, total quality school*, and others to explain this movement. These terms emphasize a focus on factors such as the customer, stakeholder, systems management, collaborative leadership style, teamwork, a belief in the continuous improvement philosophy, and a commitment to quality. The Malcolm Baldrige National Quality Award Criteria for Performance Excellence also addresses each of these factors through a set of well-researched management criteria that all types of business, education, and

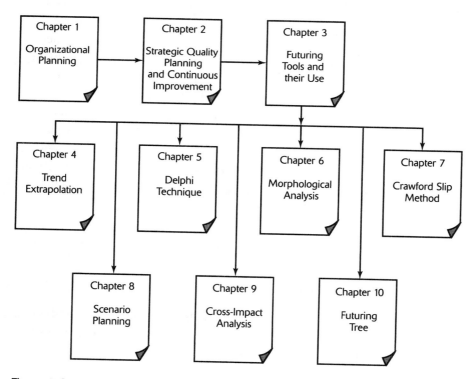

Figure 1. Organization of *Futuring Tools for Strategic Quality Planning In Education*.

health care organizations are using to achieve meaningful change and important organizational results.

It is through the continuous improvement philosophy and its principles that the abilities of the educational leader are enhanced and the synergistic potential of the human resources in the organization is released.

The organization of this book is shown graphically in Figure 1. The first three chapters provide a discussion of the need for more systematic ways to develop an organization's strategic future. They build a fundamental knowledge of planning and the continuous improvement philosophy.

The remaining chapters present a selection of seven futuring tools and techniques with a step-by-step procedure on how to use each of them. A general overview of each chapter is given as follows.

Chapter 1, "Organizational Planning," provides an explanation of the need for planning and a summary of long-range, tactical, and short-range planning. Strategic planning and its hierarchical relationship with these plans is also described. The chapter defines future planning terms followed by future timelines and their implications. The chapter concludes with a rationale for the importance of strategic quality planning.

Chapter 2, "Strategic Quality Planning and Continuous Improvement," links the philosophy of continuous improvement prevalent in the quality movement with strategic planning. It compares the concept of continuous improvement through KAIZEN with that of the western culture. It also explains the value of strategic thinking and describes the procedure for strategic quality planning in education. The chapter concludes with a summary of deployment planning.

Chapter 3, "Futuring Tools and their Use," introduces a set of practical futuring tools that may be used by organizational teams to develop a vision and strategic future. The chapter explains how these tools interrelate and how they may be applied in the strategic quality planning process.

Chapter 4, "Trend Extrapolation," describes a tool that identifies, collects, and analyzes trend patterns of the past and present, extrapolates these trends and determines their probable impact on an organization.

Chapter 5, "Delphi Technique," explains the process of selecting and surveying a group of experts to determine a probable future for an organization. This is accomplished through a sequence of questionnaires directed at the expert group, whose responses are condensed and narrowed until a specific future forecast is obtained.

Chapter 6, "Morphological Analysis," describes a tool that develops several creative solutions by analyzing each parameter and element in a sequence of events, brainstorming alternative ideas for each event, and then connecting the alternatives to create a new solution.

Chapter 7, "Crawford Slip Method," presents a tool used for gathering large amounts of information and ideas, organizing these around central themes, prioritizing the themes, and developing an action plan for implementation.

Chapter 8, "Scenario Planning," presents a tool that analyzes and develops one or more scenarios describing the possible futures of an organization based upon selected predetermined and uncertain factors.

Chapter 9, "Cross-Impact Analysis," describes a tool used to discover and analyze the interrelationships between and among future events and employs probability to determine the likelihood that the events will occur as forecast or be affected by other factors.

Chapter 10, "Futuring Tree," describes a tool that begins with a projected future state and then works backward through a branch point network of alternative pathways to connect the organization's future with its present state. The analysis passes through several phases in the process of linking the future with the present.

Using *Futuring Tools for Strategic Quality Planning in Education* can be an enriching way to look at the future of your organization. Enjoy your journey in preparing for the future. It can be rewarding and lead to an immense level of satisfaction as you watch your organization move into the future with an organized strategic quality plan.

Reference

Malcolm Baldrige National Quality Award Criteria for Performance Excellence. 1998. Gaithersburg, MD: National Institute of Standards and Technology.

Acknowledgments

The authors wish to acknowledge the following people and organizations that have provided information and inspiration for pursuing this book.

To W. Edwards Deming, for his vision of leadership and inspiration to manage organizations through the philosophy of continuous quality improvement;

To Quality Education New Jersey (QENJ) and its parent organization, Quality New Jersey (QNJ), for their persistent efforts to improve education through implementation of continuous quality improvement and by bringing together collaborative groups from education, business, industry, health care, and government to find ways to improve the future of education;

To the Cherry Hill School District and The College of New Jersey, who have provided examples of quality improvement initiatives and given support for the time and research necessary to prepare this manuscript;

And most importantly, to our families who have been so patient, and in particular, our wives, Kathy and Terry, who have given their love, support, and assistance to make this happen. To them goes our deepest appreciation.

About the Authors

William F. Alexander, Ed.D.

Dr. William Alexander is Professor of Educational Administration and Director of the Institute for Quality Improvement at The College of New Jersey. He has been directly involved with the total quality improvement initiatives on campus.

Dr. Alexander served three years on the National Quality in Education Consortium, helping to develop and conduct the National Quality Symposium offered in West Virginia, California, Pennsylvania, and Missouri. He has been active with the Education Focus Group on Quality in New Jersey and has served on the Executive Board of Quality New Jersey (QNJ) and the Governing Board of Continuous Improvement of Education in New Jersey (CIENJ). He was instrumental in forming the New Jersey Higher Education Roundtable and has served as chair. He holds membership in a number of quality organizations including the American Society for Quality (ASQ), the Association for Quality Participation, (AQP), the Association for Supervision and Current Development (ASCD), the National Quality in Education Committee (NQEC), Quality New Jersey (QNJ), the Philadelphia Area Council for Excellence (PACE), and the state committee to develop the New Jersey Quality Achievement Award in Education.

He is an examiner for the New Jersey Quality Achievement Award in the industry and education areas and has recently been trained as an evaluator for the Malcolm Baldrige National Quality Award in Education sponsored by the National Institute for Standards and Technology, United States

Department of Commerce. He participated in a site visit to one of the two qualifying applicants in 1995.

Dr. Alexander received his bachelor's degree from the University of Maine at Gorham. The master's and doctoral degrees were earned from the Pennsylvania State University. He has been a guest lecturer at several colleges and universities and received a Fulbright Scholarship for research and teaching at the Johann W. Goethe Universität in Frankfurt, Germany.

Richard W. Serfass, Ed.D.

Dr. Richard Serfass is the Executive Director of QNJ, a nonprofit organization whose mission is to encourage the application of quality management philosophies and methods in all organizations in New Jersey. QNJ works with business, service, health care, government, and education organizations. He is the former Assistant Superintendent for Educational Services in Cherry Hill, New Jersey, and was in that position for fifteen years before recently retiring. While Assistant Superintendent, his responsibilities included curriculum, instruction, professional development, and assessment programs. He has served as an elementary and high school principal, high school assistant principal, and mathematics teacher. He was also an Adjunct Professor at the Rowan College of New Jersey and The College of New Jersey, and is currently teaching at St. Joseph's University as an Adjunct Professor.

Dr. Serfass is actively involved in applying the principles of total quality management (TQM) in educational settings, the central office, the school, and the classroom. He spent the 1993–1994 year on sabbatical as Executive Administrator for a New Jersey school/business partnership known as Quality Education New Jersey where he served as co-chair for two years. He has developed and taught TQM courses at Trenton State College and served as evaluator on the Malcolm Baldrige National Quality Award in Education Pilot Evaluation Team for two years. Dr. Serfass has coordinated the program that developed the New Jersey Quality Achievement Award in education and is an examiner for the state award process.

Dr. Serfass has given state and national presentations in the areas of Strategic Quality Planning, Futuring, Program Evaluation and Development, and Total Quality Management Concepts in Education. He has authored several articles, among them *One District's Quality Improvement Story, Empowering Students to Learn in a Quality Classroom,* and *Using Standards to Foster Educational Transformation.*

Dr. Serfass received his bachelor's degree in mathematics from LaSalle College and his M.Ed. and Ed.D. in Educational Administration from Temple University. He was the President of the New Jersey Association for Supervision and Curriculum Development (NJASCD) in 1994–1995, is a current member of the Board of Directors of International ASCD, and a member of a number of professional educational organizations related to education and quality.

List of Figures

Chapter 1

Organizational Planning

"To prophesy is extremely difficult—especially with respect to the future."

—Author Unknown

Developing a strategic future is important for an organization's effectiveness and survival. However, determining the future through a systematic process of forecasting and visioning is not well known nor widely practiced in education.

From Intuition to Data-Based Planning

Educators who rely on entrepreneurial intuition or crystal ball gazing to forecast their future usually do not have sufficient knowledge of the present situation nor a clear understanding of the past and are unlikely to produce a reliable future forecast. Many organizations use brainstorming, trial and error, trend tracking, executive mandate and other such methods to seek out a future for the organization. The danger of these approaches to futuring is that they are neither systematic nor systemic to the organization. Future projections in this context are not unlike past recollections in that the farther they get from the present, the less reliable they become.

For instance, an innovation in product design may be marketed by a company on a trial and error basis only to find that the product does not satisfy the customer, as in the case of the new Coke II produced by The Coca-Cola Bottling Company. The television entertainment industry brainstorms new shows for fall preview and then watches the ratings to determine which ones to keep and which to drop.

In the government sector, much of the future planning is done by executive order or through government committees that work within the political and economic parameters imposed on them. For example, candidates for local, state, and national political offices have platforms that present their beliefs regarding what needs to be improved and how this should be done. The original version is often filtered through political debate and compromise, resulting in a plan for improvement that is quite different from the original. Examples of this are changes in health care programs, international trade agreements, shifts in political priorities from regulation to deregulation, restructuring of the military in the post–Cold War era, and establishment of national standards for education. All of these are influenced by the political process and the nation's economic priorities.

In the educational sector, future planning seems to be provoked by critics and supporters alike who are searching for answers to questions such as, Where is education headed? Are we too traditional? What will the future be like? and Why must we change? The myriad constraints imposed by taxpayers, school boards, state departments of education, fiscal laws, and resources, combined with the challenges presented by a variety of individual visionaries, pose a number of problems to educational leaders.

There seem to be two primary categories of educational leaders: (1) those who are driven by tradition through executive decision making and top-down authority; and (2) those who monitor student and stakeholder needs and respond to them to maintain constancy of purpose. Leaders in the first category are becoming increasingly ineffective due to the rapid changes in the economic, technical, political, and social-cultural fabric of our society, and are not addressed in this book. Educational leaders in the second category are more sensitive to student and stakeholder requirements and often assume an entrepreneurial leadership style to create products or services that are unexpected and delightful to the student and stakeholder. This requires a great deal of risk taking. Leaders who engage in this are called *trailblazers*. People in their institutions set new standards, create new ideas, wrestle with what works and what doesn't, and are engaged in continuous incremental change. Schools in the first category tend to benchmark those in the second group to learn from their efforts and investments.

Types of Organizational Planning

"If we continue to do things the way we have always done them, we are likely to get the results we have always gotten." This anonymous statement focuses directly on the problem. Education has experienced myriad innovations and creative ideas over the years, only to find we continually return to what seems to work best for us, that is, our traditional ways of doing things. It appears that education is entering a period in which the voices of reform are now loud enough to gain the attention of its stakeholders, including the political leaders and Congress of the United States. State and national governments, in concert with appropriate professional associations, are urging educators to conduct future planning to guide schools in achieving more efficient practices.

Educational leaders engage in several forms of planning to keep their organizations current and competitive, most of which are driven by external requirements. For example, school districts and institutions are required to have an annual plan guided by a long-range plan usually focused on a period of three to five years from the present. Many schools develop a business (tactical) plan, which complements the annual plan by aligning resources. Descriptions of these and other planning recommendations for educators are provided in Figure 1-1.

Long-Range Planning

Long-range planning is done at the district or institution level to develop key goals, objectives, and strategies for the next three to five years. Current trends within the organization are examined and compared with projected trends in the external environment to establish direction. Its focus is to identify and plan for organizational changes necessary to remaining current and competitive. The results of this planning are the formulation of long-term goals and objectives. These goals and objectives are developed by a planning committee or come from a strategic plan. They are sequenced on an annual basis to form the framework of the annual plan. This establishes the direction for the organization. See example in Figure 1-1.

The long-range plan also determines how the organization's goals, objectives, and strategies are deployed throughout the district and how they are linked to the business and annual plans.

Strategic Initiatives	Long-Range Goals	Objectives	Strategies
Year 1			
I. Conduct comprehensive analysis of community needs and program/curricula needs.	A. Conduct community needs assessment and analyze for program/curricula needs.	A-1. Establish a district-wide advisory committee to guide the development of needs assessment criteria, process, and reporting. A-2. Conduct community-wide needs assessment involving appropriate offices and agencies within and outside the community.	Determine the demographic composition of the community and any changes that have taken place that will require change in district programs/curricula.
	B. Restructure programs and curricula.	B-1. Analyze current programs for compliance. B-2. Develop or revise program/curricula to meet needs. B-3. Create a climate for change within the community.	Involve parents, stakeholders, and school personnel in the analysis.
II. Form partnerships with appropriate businesses and industries, agencies, and special groups in the greater community.	C. Form partnerships with community constituents to garner support and assistance in meeting community needs.	C-1. Develop guidelines and criteria for forming partnerships.	Establish a task force from within the advisory group to research potential partners for the district.

Figure 1-1. Sample long-range goals and objectives.

Year 2		
III. Plan for School-Based Management (SBM).	A. Prepare principals and administrators for the transition from central to school-based management.	A-1. Conduct research on school-based management and prepare report.
		A-2. Prepare training sessions for administrators on SBM.
		A-3. Establish experimental site for implementing SBM.
		Benchmark other districts that have implemented school-based management successfully.
IV. Adopt year-round schools.	B. Establish experimental year-round school(s) in district.	B-1. Study the feasibility of 12-month schools in terms of resources and personnel.
		Benchmark other districts that have been successful. Involve parents and community.

Year 3		
V. Review areas for program expansion to more effectively achieve goals.		
VI. Install current instructional technology for students and faculty to access Internet, to provide home instruction through distance learning, and other state-of-the-art uses.		

Year 4		
VII. Develop Workforce-Career Education Programs.		

Year 5		
VIII. Assess district performance in meeting goals and objectives. Reassess strategic plan and initiatives.		

Figure 1-1. Sample long-range goals and objectives *(continued).*

The Business (Tactical) Plan

This is a short to intermediate range plan, usually two to three years in duration. Its function is to develop planning and budgeting strategies related to administrative and operational activities that flow from the organization's objectives. Tactical planning produces expedient action plans within the organization by aligning human, fiscal, technical, and physical resources to achieve the goals and objectives expressed in the long-range plan. Alignment of organizational resources is achieved through prioritization of requests, based upon the extent to which they support strategic and long-range goals. The tactical plan also identifies how planning components are deployed throughout the organization. See Figure 1-2.

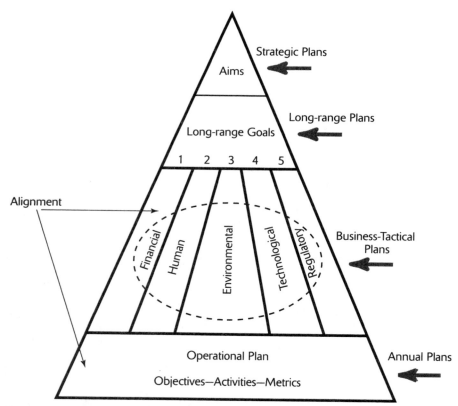

Figure 1-2. Articulating plans.

The Annual (Operational) Plan

The annual plan, sometimes called the operational plan, is a one-year plan that translates the long-range and business plans into actions on an annual basis. This plan creates strategies and activities designed to meet long-range goals and objectives. Assessment strategies are also developed and deployed throughout the plan to evaluate achievement of objectives and provide accountability for the school. See sample in Figure 1-3.

Strategic Planning

Strategic planning enables an organization to regenerate itself continuously by envisioning its future, assessing what and where it is currently, and determining what goals and strategies are necessary to move the organization toward its future. Cook (1990) suggests that "strategic planning is the means by which an organization constantly recreates itself to achieve common purpose." Once a strategic plan is developed, the organization sets processes in place to achieve the goals stated in the plan.

Goodstein et al. (1993) define strategic planning as "the process by which the guiding members of an organization envision the future and develop the necessary procedures and operations to achieve that future." Strategic planning involves assumptions about the future environments of an organization. The difference between strategic planning and long-range planning lies in the process of creating and evaluating alternative future goals based on the collection of data from the many environments that influence an organization, such as the political, social, economic, technological, geographic, legal, and demographic environments. Capon and Hulbert (1987) conclude that "the gathering of environmental information and adapting to environmental change are the primary characteristics of planning that make it strategic." Figure 1-4 shows the hierarchical planning model for education that incorporates these criteria.

Strategic planning works well when educators revisit what "business" they are in, who their customers and stakeholders are, and what these constituents need and expect. It also defines how components of the whole organization relate to each other within their internal and external environments and provides direction for, and constraints on, long-range, intermediate, and short-range planning.

Ralph Waldo Emerson once wrote, "There are always two parties, the party of the past and the party of the future; the establishment and the

Objectives	Activities	Assessment
A-1. Establish a district-wide advisory committee to guide the development of needs assessment criteria, process, and reporting.	1a. Establish an advisory committee consisting of representative members of the school and community. Members should represent business, industry, government, agencies, and offices within and outside the community. Include customers and stakeholders. Suggested membership around 20 people.	Confirm representation from cross-section of community.
	1b. Allocate resources to train committee in needs analysis procedure, criteria, data collection, and reporting.	Examine results of participation in training sessions.
A-2. Conduct community-wide needs assessment.	2a. Organize the committee structure and conduct needs assessment.	Monitor progress and results.
B-1. Analyze current programs for compliance.	1a. Compare current programs with results of needs assessment report. Identify programs that need revisions, deletion, or addition.	
B-2. Develop or revise programs or curricula to meet needs.	2a. Charge district supervisors with responsibility for reviewing and revising programs where needed.	Arrange for time and resources for this task. Distribute progress reports to main committee for review during process.
B-3. Create a climate for change within the community.	3a. Communicate results of needs assessment to community and rally support from leaders.	Survey community to ascertain climate for change.
C-1. Develop guidelines and criteria for forming partnerships.	1a. Benchmark other school districts that have been successful with partnerships.	Use established benchmark procedures.
	1b. Develop guidelines and criteria for partnering.	Compare with districts that use partnerships.

Figure 1-3. Sample section of annual plan.

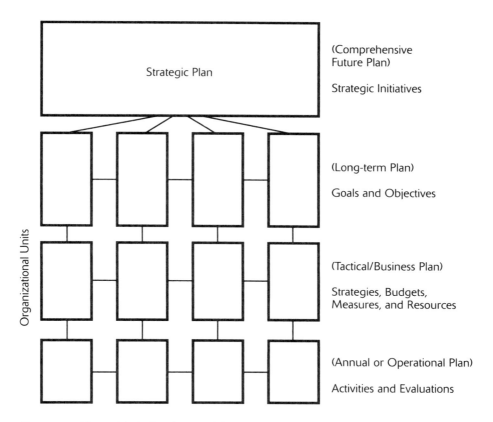

Figure 1-4. Hierarchical planning model.

movement." Strategic planning is about the movement: education's continuous struggle to plot a course through an increasingly inconsistent environment where experience is rapidly devalued and familiar landmarks no longer serve as guideposts (Hamel and Prahalad 1994).

These plans are vertically articulated to form a cohesive hierarchical process that guides the selection and deployment of goals and objectives, resource allocations, proposed activities, and assessments garnered by the business and annual plans. These plans guide the decision making and actions of the district or institution.

Future Planning

Most schools claim to have a future plan in one form or another. Many, however, refer to a long-range plan that has been developed by senior administrators and cascaded down to the departments and units within the organization. Other plans often result from a recognized need for a future plan or the task of preparing for an upcoming visit by an evaluating agency such as the National Study of School Evaluation (NSSE), the National Council for the Accreditation of Teacher Education (NCATE), the National Association of State Directors of Teacher Education Certification (NASDTEC), or other state accrediting agencies. A growing number of schools are now using the Malcolm Baldrige National Quality Award (MBNQA) in Education criteria for self-assessment. Responses to these criteria require a great deal of preparation and a broad assessment of the total district or institution. This comprehensive assessment is done internally and produces a cross-sectional profile of the organization that discloses key information targeted by the assessment criteria. The MBNQA criteria identify the need for future planning as one of their "Core Values." It is described in the *MBNQA Criteria for Performance Excellence in Education* as the "Long-range View of the Future" in the following words:

> Pursuit of education improvement requires a strong future orientation and a willingness to make long-term commitments to students and to all stakeholders—communities, employers, faculty, and staff. Planning needs to anticipate many types of changes, including changes in education requirements, instructional approaches, resource availability, technology, and demographics. A major longer-term investment associated with school improvement is the investment in creating and sustaining a mission-oriented assessment system focused on learning. This entails faculty education and training in assessment methods. It also entails school leadership becoming familiar with research findings and practical applications of assessment methods and learning style information. (MBNQA, Education 1998)

A review of current literature reveals many different terms and methods used to determine what the future may bring to an organization and how an organization forecasts its future. Terms such as forecasting, visioning, futuring, futurcasting, and predicting have been used by writers in an attempt to describe a suitable plan that will guide members of an organization toward the future of their choice. The following is a review of the terminology and timelines related to creating and developing the future of an organization.

Forecasting

Forecasting can be a relatively uncomplicated task or a highly sophisticated science. In its simplest form it has been defined as "a process which has as its objective the prediction of future events or conditions" (Levenbach and Cleary 1981). In its more complex form it may be described as a process of collecting as much information as possible about an organization, extrapolating and analyzing the impact of environmental influences on the organization, and presenting a descriptive portrait of the organization in a specified future time period. Forecasting implies the use of some means of systematic analysis.

Visioning

Vision is very important for constancy of purpose. It is one of the terms most commonly used to describe an organization's future, because that window to the future sets direction for the organization. Nanus refers to vision as a "realistic, credible, attractive future for your organization" (1992). Whitley calls vision a "vivid picture of an ambitious, desirable future state that is connected with the customer and better in some important way than the current state" (1991). These views present a creative and data-driven approach to vision development.

   Visions are not predictable, although they describe the organization's *preferred* future state. In many cases, vision alternatives must be considered, ranging from *probable* to *possible* futures. Since visions are essentially dreams or aspirations, they must be analyzed critically to examine their foundation, accuracy, and the likelihood of their achievement. The process of visioning, like forecasting, must be conducted in a systematic way to achieve best results.

Futuring

Futuring has its origin in the early studies of futurology. It describes the scientific study of the future and tries to answer the problems of the destiny of an organization. This approach is concerned with the broad impact of social, cultural, environmental, political, and technological changes that offer valuable information to forecasters. Futuring, futurism, and future studies are popular terms currently in use. Barker (1992) divides the field of future studies into two areas: *content futurism* and *process futurism*. Content futurism is concerned about the "whats" of the future; that is, what technology will look like or what the environment will look like. Process futurism focuses on "how" one arrives at the future, or how the "whats" will come about. The futuring tools discussed in this book are focused on process futurism.

Futurcasting

Kurtzman (1984) uses the term *futurcasting* as "charting a way into the future; to test alternative futures before they occur." He contrasts futurcasting with forecasting, concluding that "forecasting is concerned with studying trends to determine their probable and logical outcome, futurcasting is concerned with ways to arrive at desired outcomes and goals." There seems to be little difference in these terms beyond this point in his book.

Predicting

W. Edwards Deming has said many times that management has responsibility for prediction. He argues that prediction increases knowledge, and knowledge is the prerequisite for action. When predictions and actions coincide, this increases wisdom. In order to predict you must have data. To collect data, you must ask a question. To ask a question, you must first have a theory. Scherkenbach (1991) suggests a connection between prediction as part of a theory of knowledge and the Plan-Do-Study-Act cycle. Prediction as a future-planning term is more of an operational concept than the other terms described here. This concept is further illustrated in Figure 1-5.

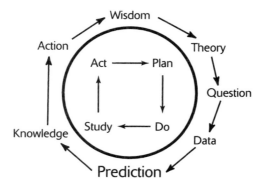

Figure 1-5. Prediction as part of the Plan-Do-Study-Act cycle.

Timelines for Future Planning

Forecasting tomorrow's weather is a lot easier than attempting a forecast for a week or a month away. The same is true for an organization. Makridakis and Wheelwright (1987) speak to the role of time ranges or time horizons as one of the factors affecting the accuracy of future planning. In their view, long-range planning for a period of greater than two years can often be inaccurate. Medium-range planning covers a three-month to two-year period, while short-range planning covers less than three months. Plans for the shorter time frames tend to be more accurate. Sullivan and Claycombe (1977) suggest the same time frames.

Future planning in a highly technological enterprise is different from that employed by a government or academic organization. In the computer chip market, for example, the rate of change in technology is staggering. Other fast-changing industries include pharmaceuticals, chemicals, and the environmental groups. The future planner in these industries needs to continually update the planning process as new data becomes available. The time frames cited above seem appropriate for these organizations.

In education, however, future planning can realistically consume a much larger time frame depending upon previous indicators in the region. Live birth data and housing starts are essential data for public education. Classroom availability, expansion capabilities, and building funds for colleges are variables that do not change as rapidly as those in the computer industry. Therefore, organizationally specific time frames need to be considered when future planning. One of the best methods is to research planning outcomes of the past, which tend to be an excellent indicator of time determination. A summary of suggested future-planning time ranges for non-rapid-change organizations such as education is shown in Figure 1-6.

The several terms described here represent a continuum of processes for developing an organization's future. The continuum ranges from creative brainstorming to serious prediction with supporting data of what the future will look like. Future planning is reflected in strategic plans developed by school districts and institutions. Strategic planning models vary throughout education in their format and process; however, the end result is usually the same. Key to working out a strategic plan are the internal and external environmental scans. As indicated earlier, these are part of the critical analysis required of visions, in order to test their accuracy and probability of occurrence. It is this systems thinking that establishes the foundation for strategic quality planning. The authors of this book take the position that the more

Range/Term	Years	Description
Short	0–1	An annual plan, good control over events. Planning easily monitored and usually successful.
Intermediate	1–3	Used to link long-range and short-range plans through tactical or business plan.
Long	3–5	Long-range planning for continuity of mission and evolutionary change through continuous improvement. Some level of control, reactions to events or trends, and direction for change.
Far	5–10	Strategic planning to provide future initiatives. Many variables, largely speculation and unreliable predictions.

Figure 1-6. Planning timelines for education.

scientific or systematic the process used in generating a future for schools, the better the probability is for realizing that future.

References

Barker, J. A. 1992. *Future Edge*. New York: William Morrow and Company, p. 21.

Bauman, P. 1996. *Governing Education: Public Sector Reform or Privatization*. Needham Heights, MA: Allyn & Bacon.

Caravatta, M. 1997. *Let's Work Smarter, Not Harder*. American Society for Quality, Milwaukee, WI: Quality Press.

Deming, W. E. 1993. *The New Economy*. Cambridge, MA: Massachusetts Institute of Technology Center for Advanced Engineering Study, p. 104–5.

Hamel, G., and C. K. Prahalad. 1994. *Competing for the Future*. Boston, MA: Harvard Business School Press, p. ix, 82.

Hanson, E. M. 1996. *Educational Administration and Organizational Behavior*. 4th ed. Needham Heights, MA: Allyn & Bacon.

Hesselbein, F., M. Goldsmith, and R. Beckhard. 1996. *The Leader of the Future*. New York: The Drucker Foundation.

Joseph, E. C. 1974. "An Introduction to Studying the Future," *Futurism in Education*. Berkeley, CA: McCutchen Publishing Corporation, p. 2–3, 11.

Kurtzman, J. 1984. *Futurcasting*. Palm Springs, CA: ETC Publications, p. i–ii.

Levelback, H., and J. P. Cleary. 1981. *The Beginning Forecaster: The Forecasting Process through Data Analysis*. Belmont, CA: Lifetime Learning Publications, p. 3.

Makridakis, S., and S. C. Wheelwright. 1987. *The Handbook of Forecasting: A Manager's Guide*. New York: John Wiley & Sons p. 12–14.

Malcolm Baldrige National Quality Award Criteria for Performance Excellence in Education. 1998. Gaithersburg, MD: National Institute for Standards and Technology.

Nanus, B. 1992. *Visionary Leadership*. San Francisco: Jossey-Bass, p. 8.

Scherkenbach, W. 1991. *Deming's Road to Continual Improvement*. Knoxville: SPC Press, p. 196.

Sullivan, W. G., and W. W. Claycombe. 1977. *Fundamentals of Forecasting*. Reston, VA: Reston Publishing Company, p. 3.

Whitley, R. C. 1991. *The Customer-Driven Company: Moving from Talk to Action*. Reading, MA: Addison-Wesley Publishing Company, p. 26.

Chapter 2

Strategic Quality Planning and Continuous Improvement

"It is always wise to look ahead, but difficult to look further than you can see."

—Winston Churchill

Strategic quality planning is important to the future of an organization. It is clear that the time periods of the past and present are fixed. It is the future that offers opportunity for change. The past offers evidence to help us better understand situations that exist today, whereas the present contains the forces that will frame the future. Thus, if organizations desire to change or to be different in some way, they must systematically seek out those forces lurking in the present and develop a plan that will incorporate them into their future. This is accomplished through strategic planning.

Strategic Planning

Educational planners have relied heavily on long-range and operational planning for decades. Usually these have been developed at the school board, board of trustees, and senior staff levels, and handed down to appropriate units and departments for deployment. Another form of planning also gained popularity in industry and found its way into education in the 1970s through a small number of administrative entrepreneurs who believed in the necessity of planning for the future to ensure constancy of purpose. This was identified as strategic planning.

Definition

According to McCune (1986) strategic planning is "a process for organizational renewal and transformation. This process provides a means of matching services and activities with changed and changing environmental conditions . . . [It] provides a framework for the improvement and restructuring of programs, management, collaborations, and evaluation of the organization's progress." Organizations that have the following characteristics will experience better success with strategic planning: (1) they determine their own identity, (2) they are autonomous, (3) they acquire and allocate resources, (4) they have vision and supporting leadership, and (5) they are responsible for planning (Cook 1990).

The Strategic Planning category of the MBNQA examines how the school sets strategic direction, how the school develops key action plans to support the directions, how the school's strategy and action plans are deployed, and how school performance is tracked and projected into the future (MBNQA, Education 1998).

A practical model for strategic planning in education is shown in Figure 2-1. The Y-shape model was chosen because of the three major considerations required for planning: (1) *Where are you now?* (2) *Where do you want to be?* and (3) *How do you get there?*

Where Are You Now?

This question asks for your purpose or reason for existence (usually expressed in a mission statement) and your organization's shared values. A strategic planning team should be established and charged with finding answers to these questions. The team should consist of representatives from all major functions of the district or institution. A team of 12 to 18 members is not uncommon. Representatives should reflect the district or institutional personnel, community leaders, parents, students, and other stakeholders. Before the team assumes responsibility for future planning, they must receive training in how to work as a team and be well oriented to the assigned task.

A number of public school districts, colleges, and universities identify and publish a mission statement describing their purpose and raison d'etre.

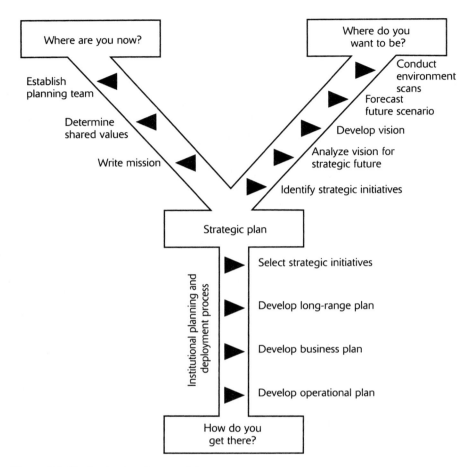

Figure 2-1. Strategic planning model.

This mission comes from the organization's *canon* and is supported by the shared values of the membership. One of the team functions is to survey the member values, analyze them, and ascertain those values that are shared within the organization. These form the standard of practice required to meet the organization's mission. Examples of shared value statements are:

• We value diversity—we will actively promote an atmosphere of mutual respect for each other's differences, recognizing that our diversity creates a breadth of perspectives that strengthens our organization.

- We value communication—open, candid communication flowing in all directions will be the norm. We emphasize that listening is a crucial component of the communication process. (*Corestates Bank of Delaware*)

The mission statement is very important to an organization, for it provides a clear and concise description of its purpose and function. Three questions must be answered when formulating a mission. They are: (1) What is the main purpose and function of your organization? (2) Who are the primary customers and stakeholders of your organization? and (3) What do these customers/stakeholders consider as value-added service? Once the mission statement has been drafted and distributed for feedback, it is ready for general consensus and publication. Examples of mission statements from the K–12 and higher education sectors are:

- The Pinellas County School District unites with families and the community in using continual quality improvement to provide a foundation for life that enables and challenges all students to be successful in a global and multicultural society. (Pinellas County Florida 1993)

- The mission of the Cherry Hill Public Schools is to provide a quality educational program in a positive environment preparing its students to be knowledgeable, responsible, caring, and confident citizens in an ever-changing world. (Cherry Hill New Jersey Public Schools 1995)

- To develop, transmit, and utilize knowledge to educate scholars and leaders for the state of Indiana and the nation. (MBNQA Midstate University Case Study 1995)

Following approval of the mission, key strategies and activities are developed to accomplish the mission. Assessment procedures and instruments are also developed to measure achievement. Organizations may set goals around their mission and pursue accomplishment of these goals as a measure of success. Missions, however, are oriented to the present. Goals established from the mission focus on the present, creating organizational myopia. Without vision, there is no positive direction established toward the future. Rather, the organization is left to drift. Many schools reach the level of mission and go directly to the development of their long-range and annual plans.

These schools do not invest in future planning and therefore perpetuate the status quo.

Where Do You Want to Be?

To answer this question, the team projects a vision and strategic aims for the organization by scanning the internal and external environmental influences. This examination results in the identification of the organization's internal strengths and weaknesses as well as those external threats and opportunities relevant to reaching the desired future. The environmental scanning includes an analysis of those external forces that will have an impact on the organization's future.

Scanning the *internal* environment is done to determine the organization's key internal strengths and weaknesses. The planning team will critically examine such things as the organization's culture; its management, staff, faculty, and governance; its instructional programs, curriculums, financial resources, technology and community relations; its rituals, rights, and traditions; its communication processes and networks; its shared values, mission, goals, and objectives; and its success in meeting customer/stakeholder requirements. From this examination will come a list of strengths and weaknesses.

Scanning the *external* environment requires a careful analysis of those demographic, economic, political, social-cultural, technological, educational, and of course those competitive trends and forces that will impact the organization's future. This process involves collecting data on trends, innovations, and projections by futurists and intuitive leaders. It results in the realization of external threats and opportunities that will influence the future of the organization. With this knowledge, the planning team can proceed to develop a scenario of what the future might look like. The vision is created from this scenario.

The key component of this area of concern is vision. According to Peter Senge (1990), "visions without systems thinking ends up painting lovely pictures of the future with no deep understanding of the forces that must be mastered to move from here to there." The method used to generate a vision may result in two or more alternative futures. It is important that organizations understand the meaning of alternative futures and think in terms of visions that may be *plausible*, those that are *possible*, those that are *probable*, and of course those that are most desirable or *preferred* (Fitch and Svengalis 1979). Selection of the appropriate futuring tool or technique must be done with caution to ensure realistic rather than idealistic vision. Whether organi-

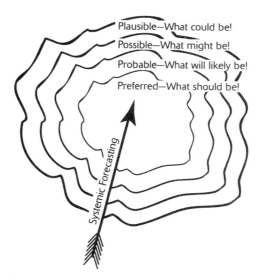

Figure 2-2. Alternative visions.

zations use creative futuring or systematic futuring tools, they should understand the procedures required for their use and be skilled in their applications. See Figure 2-2.

When the first two considerations are answered satisfactorily, the strategic plan is taking shape. The final action is to identify clearly the strategic initiatives that will be selected, sequenced, and translated into goals and objectives for the long-range plan. The plan is then communicated to the organizational membership for approval and commitment.

How Do You Get There?

The third consideration is *How do you get there?* It is at this point in the process that strategic initiatives are selected for long-range planning. Realizing that not all initiatives may be achievable right away, the school or district must select and sequence them by focusing on those that are achievable during the three-to-five-year long-range plan. As the initiatives are accomplished, others are selected and a revised long-term plan is developed and implemented. Examples of strategic initiatives are:

- Decentralize administration through site-based management.

- Develop language and multicultural programs to accommodate growing immigrant populations.

- Establish a program of international studies in business administration and education.

The major task at this point is to select those initiatives that can reasonably be accomplished during the first year, second year, and so on. They are built into the long-term plan and deployed throughout the organization both vertically and horizontally. This may be done through Hoshin Planning (the Japanese process for "policy deployment," or simply the means by which targets are reached) or by the American version called "quality function deployment." Figure 1-4 in chapter 1 illustrates a simplified model for deploying strategic initiatives. These initiatives are then translated into goals and objectives for the long-range plan. The tactical plan generates strategies, resources, priorities, budgets, and measures to prepare for the long-range commitment. This process is illustrated in the articulation model in Figure 1-2. The operational plan focuses on the initiatives, goals, strategies, and objectives selected and develops activities for the objectives and strategies, and also evaluates their effectiveness in accomplishing the strategic initiatives.

Strategic Quality Planning

Strategic quality planning imposes additional steps to strengthen that arm of the Y-model that asks *Where do you want to be?* The four steps in this part of the model focus on vision as its montage of the future; that is, conducting environmental scans, forecasting rough scenario, developing vision, and identifying strategic aims. As indicated earlier, vision is a dream or aspiration for the future of an organization. A vision developed with knowledge of the internal and external forces that are likely to act on it has a higher probability of materializing. It is this type of thinking that leads planners to an organization's strategic quality future. Examining the forces affecting visions provides better control of the preferred future. Vision, then, becomes the window to an organization's strategic quality future.

Strategic quality planning may be described as the incorporation of the principles of strategic planning and the quality management philosophy to produce a data-driven forecast that has high validity and probability of occurring. It overlays a systemic quality on visioning. It is a systematic approach to forecasting that employs research, discussion, assessment, analysis, and consensus to approximate, with a high degree of confidence, what the organization will be doing in the future time zone selected.

Strategic quality planning is concerned with those forces acting on vision both before and after it is developed. Visions must be examined and analyzed critically to ascertain the nature and impact of those forces that are likely to affect them from the time of inception until the future time period in which they are to be achieved. Unexamined visions are often affected by (1) the interrelationships of their components; (2) the nature of the influence of these interrelationships, whether positive or negative; (3) the sequential manner in which the vision components emerge or begin to form; and (4) the strength of the influence. One might view this process as "filtering the vision." Figure 2-3 suggests a model for filtering a vision through several criteria including the internal and external environmental scans; benchmarking and vision sharing; analysis of interrelationships; and those tactical considerations that align organizational resources and drive the organization toward its proposed future. The result is a strategic quality future.

For example, suppose a school district or college decided to use the Trend Extrapolation futuring tool described in chapter 4. This tool identifies baseline trends, traces their historical applications over the past three or four decades, and summarizes current trends. Internal and external environmental scans are conducted on these trends, which identify internal strengths and weaknesses and external threats and opportunities. Given this information, current trends are then extrapolated five to ten years into the future to predict a cluster of events, activities, and conditions that might prevail at the projected future time. These events, activities, and conditions

Figure 2-3. A vision filter.

may be prioritized or examined to identify those that will have a significant impact on the organization's future. This result is called the forecast, which is refined into a vision.

Most organizations end the analysis here, post their vision, and proceed to develop initiatives, goals, objectives, and the conventional levels of planning. Strategic quality planning requires that you go beyond the vision by analyzing critically what could happen among the components between now and the projected time frame set to achieve the vision. For instance, what are the interrelationships between and among the events, activities, and conditions set forth in the vision? How will these interrelationships affect each other by the time the projected vision is reached? Will the effects be positive or negative? What will be the magnitude of the impact?

The Cross-Impact Analysis tool described in chapter 9 is designed to answer these questions. The tool uses a matrix to compare the effects of each event, activity, or condition against each other. These effects are weighted and result in numerical measures that are easily compared. Figure 2-4 presents a sample cluster of events listed in a vision for an urban school district. These events appear simple on the surface. When analyzed critically, however, they may change significantly based on answers to the previous questions. You may want to review chapter 9 to better understand the complete process, and how the probability of change within the vision statement is generated.

Another filter to consider is benchmarking and vision sharing. Educational organizations as a whole have not yet established common data banks of information from which to benchmark. It seems that each district, college, or institution has developed its own future plans which tend to be "in-house" documents and not readily available for other organizations to benchmark. Attempts to create data banks are well underway presently and will provide assistance to educators at a later date. Educators are not shy when it comes to sharing information with other schools. Although not a formalized process, vision sharing is commonly observed by those schools or districts that have added strategic planning to their overall planning process. Benchmarking and vision sharing form collaborative relationships among educators and allow each to benefit from the experiences of others, and to adjust visions to meet forces not considered when their vision was first developed.

Tactical considerations are another factor that will influence vision. Once the vision has been analyzed for interrelationships, internal and external forces, and benchmarking information, the organization needs to consider

If this event occurs:	The effect on on this event would be . . .				
	E1	E2	E3	E4	E5
E1 Shifts in student enrollments due to a school voucher system and increased expansion of other types of schools such as magnet and alternative schools, charter schools, and competition from private schools.	▓				
E2 Broad implementation of school-to-work transition programs developed collaboratively through industry and education partnerships.		▓			
E3 State and federal funding for urban schools remain relatively stable and proportionate to needs over the next ten years.			▓		
E4 Community-controlled schools are formed through site-based management and governed by local advisory groups composed of parents, teachers, administrators, and community stakeholders.				▓	
E5 Schools became educational, cultural, and recreational centers in their communities providing a variety of preschool, afternoon, and evening activities for all community members.					▓

Figure 2-4. Sample cross-impact matrix.

the need for adjustments in the vision that have been discovered through the filtering process. Paramount to these vision changes are the tactical requirements. For instance, the budget prioritization process may need change, human resources may need realignment, improved technology systems may need to be added, facilities may need to be added or modified, and the management-leadership may need to be reoriented to different ways of managing the school or district. This calls for realigning resources, possibly investigating new sources of financial assistance, forming partnerships with business and industry, and working more collaboratively with the parents and community. The extent to which these tactical considerations can be initiated will affect the vision. This second effort to go beyond the original vision, to analyze critically the vision and prepare to act upon the results of the analysis, is called the strategic quality future. The strategic quality future is better focused, more accurate, and more predictable than other methods, and brings the organization closer to its preferred vision of the future.

The final action in strategic quality planning is to bridge the gap between the present state and the future state of the organization. The reader is referred to the Futuring Tree described in chapter 10. This tool explains the process of linking the present with the future by starting with the future state and working backwards through several phases until connections are made with the present state of the organization. A network of priority pathways are formulated that provide the direction for the connections.

Continuous Improvement

Once the strategic quality future has been projected for an organization, the goals and strategies for achieving that future state must be identified. This is accomplished through the long-range, intermediate, and short-range plans. Continuous improvement must be part of the plans.

Deming advises organizations to create constancy of purpose toward improvement of their products and services, in order to continue to satisfy customer and stakeholder requirements. The significance of Deming's advice is to encourage organizations to commit to a plan that provides for continuous improvement in all units of the organization. An example of this is the dedication of resources to research and innovation for improving the organization's methods. It is not uncommon, however, to find an organization with a vision statement, but little or no activity to move the organization toward that vision. There is an anonymous anecdote from World War II that describes a large number of tanks moving across a desert. The lead tank stopped suddenly, halting the entire column. The commander approached the lead tank driver and asked why they had stopped. The driver replied that he had come to the end of his map and did not know which way to go from there.

In this situation, it may be assumed that either there was no continuation plan or, if there were such a plan, it was not communicated down through the organizational structure to the persons who needed to know about it. Hence, constancy of purpose as an organization-wide effort did not take place.

Continuous Improvement and Alignment

Scherkenback (1988) elaborates on Deming's principle of constancy of purpose in his discussion of variation. He points out that the principle implies more than changing products, services, or processes. He raises the importance of *alignment* throughout the organization. Alignment is a concept directly associated with variation. Scherkenback argues that variation in any of an organization's functions must be reduced and brought under control. This must be part of the continuous improvement strategy. The range of *dispersion* (a statistical phrase depicting the scattering of values of a variable around a mean or measure of central tendency of a distribution) is an indicator of the ability of an organization to control variation. When people in the organization tend to "play out" their perceived roles, doing their best, but not having a clear direction on what they should be doing, dispersion increases. This contributes heavily to inefficiency. If alignment is achieved within the organization, however, the spread of dispersion is decreased and constancy of purpose is increased. Figure 2-5 shows graphically how alignment is increased by reducing dispersion.

A more holistic concept of continuous improvement is embodied in the Japanese term KAIZEN. The fundamental meaning of KAIZEN is continuous incremental improvement. The concept permeates the organizational culture and includes everyone in it. It implies that improvement is a way of life—be it our work life, our social life, or our home life (Imai 1986). This multi-faceted concept has enabled Japanese management to take a systematic and collaborative approach to cross-functional problem solving not yet common to our western culture.

In his discussion of KAIZEN, Imai makes a distinction between strategies used in Japan and those used in the western cultures. He explains that western cultures generally rely on innovations in products, services, and processes to initiate improvement. As innovative ideas are developed and implemented, change occurs in spurts and may appear sporadic over time. This strategy, sometimes referred to as quantum leap thinking, requires abrupt changes in facilities, equipment, people, and resources, which incurs considerable costs at the time of implementation.

In contrast, KAIZEN strategy is to employ gradual, incremental, and continuous improvement as new ideas are developed. By doing this, organizations achieve continued success. It is somewhat like the phrase, "if it ain't broke, improve it." The implication is that once an organization has reached

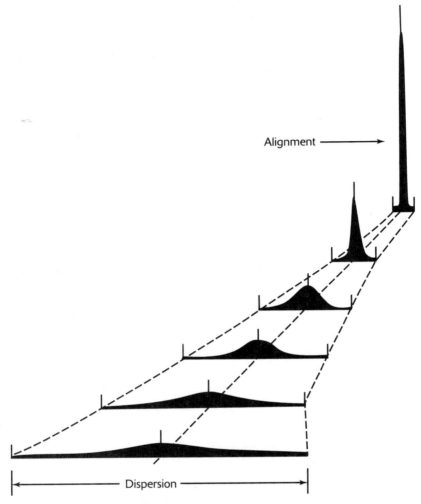

Figure 2-5. Dispersion and alignment.

its operational peak it becomes stagnant and begins to decline. Therefore a continuous, perhaps incessant effort for improvement must be provided in order to maintain at least the status quo.

Imai compares the two strategies of innovation to a staircase and a slope. Innovation produces futuristic changes in the pattern of a staircase progression. The normal operations of an organization may be approximated as a horizontal line on a chart. When an innovation is implemented

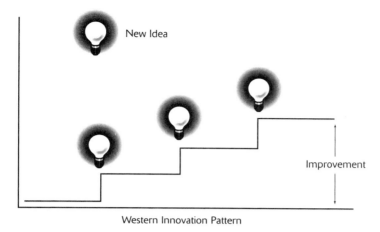

New Idea

Improvement

Western Innovation Pattern

Improvement

KAIZEN Pattern of Continuous Incremental Improvement

Figure 2-6. Patterns of continuous improvement.

there is a growth spurt indicated by a vertical line that eventually levels off as the new quality standard is achieved, producing a staircase pattern. KAIZEN, on the other hand, provides gradual change, as represented by the steady line of a slope. See Figure 2-6. It is this systemic quality of KAIZEN that is significant to the principle of continuous improvement.

Reengineering Improvement

A revolutionary concept for improving organizational performance has been introduced called *reengineering*. Although initially focused on applications in corporations, its usefulness has been extended to other organizations. Reengineering is a bold approach to change that essentially requires removing what presently exists and focusing on what the organization should be. Reengineering means starting over. Formally defined, it is "the fundamental rethinking and radical design of business processes to achieve dramatic improvements in critical, contemporary measures of performance such as cost, quality, service, and speed" (Hammer and Champy 1993). See Figure 2-7.

Although the concept of reengineering contraposes the idea of continuous incremental improvement, both approaches require changing processes to improve how work gets done in an organization. Both approaches propose a shift in thinking away from *task-based thinking,*which reflects the philosophies of early economic innovators like Adam Smith, Alfred Sloan, and Frederick Taylor, toward the *process-based thinking* represented in the more recent philosophies of continuous quality improvement evolved by Deming, Juran, Feigenbaum, Crosby, and others. Some feel that reengineering is the penalty for lack of continuous improvement.

According to the reengineering concept, altering or tinkering with existing processes that have low productivity is a waste of time. One area that is

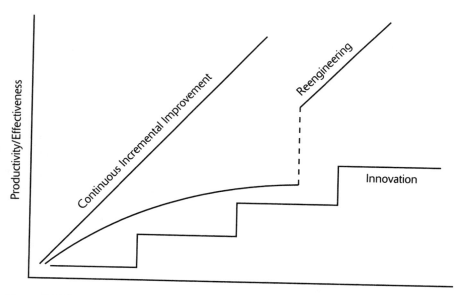

Figure 2-7. Comparison of the innovation approach, reengineering, and continuous incremental improvement.

prone to endless tinkering is our educational system. Since the publication of *A Nation At Risk* in 1983, innovations such as peer tutoring, alternative schools, cooperative learning, portfolio assessment, outcomes assessment, school to work transition, youth apprenticeship training, school-based management, and a multitude of additional schemes to improve urban education have been implemented to improve the learning process, with little success. As indicated in the *Goals 2000 Project*, the reformers would suggest reengineering American education by establishing national standards and inviting states to develop innovative schools appropriate to the twenty-first century.

The decision whether to use reengineering or continuous improvement is influenced by three factors: (1) the productivity level of process performance, (2) the time available to make changes in the processes, and (3) the organization's ability to restructure, based on its internal and external resources as well as influences. Reengineering is more likely to be used on processes that are antiquated, slow, costly, troublesome, and relatively nonproductive. If a study of the process were conducted and concluded that incremental improvement would not create the necessary change(s) in the process, due to the amount of time it would take to bring the process into alignment with the rest of the organization, reengineering should be considered.

In some instances, however, a process that is reasonably productive now may become obsolete in the near future as the organization pursues its vision. This situation would also suggest reengineering. Under normal circumstances, continuous incremental improvement will keep the process productive and competitive.

The relationship between continuous improvement and strategic quality planning is significant. Once the future state of the organization has been identified, its leaders must plan continuous incremental improvement strategies to move the organization toward its future. This has to be done very carefully because of the risk of wasting time and resources and not reaching the desired future state.

Chapter 3 describes a set of futuring tools that may be used to forecast an organization's strategic quality future. These tools use a systematic process for helping organizations to identify a basic forecast or vision, to examine critically the vision components for interrelationships and influences, and to guide the process of developing a network of priority pathways to connect the future state with the organization's present state.

References

Capon, N., and J. M. Hulbert. 1987. "Forecasting and Strategic Planning," *The Handbook of Forecasting*. New York: John Wiley & Sons, p. 75–79.

Cherry Hill Public Schools. February 1995. *Report of the Cherry Hill Public Schools' Strategic Planning Committee*. Cherry Hill, NJ, p. 2.

Cook, W. J. Jr. 1990. *Strategic Planning*. Washington, D.C.: American Association of School Administrators, p. 5, 71–75.

Corestates Bank of Delaware. Undated. *Core Values*. Wilmington, DE: The Corestates Bank.

Cunningham, W., and D. Gresso. 1994. *Cultural Leadership: The Culture of Excellence in Education*. Needham Heights, MA: Allyn & Bacon.

Deming, W. E. 1986. *Out Of The Crisis*. Cambridge, MA: Massachusetts Institute of Technology, p. 23.

Goodstein, L. P., T. Nolan, and J. W. Pfiffer. 1993. *Applied Strategic Planning*. New York: McGraw Hill, p. 3.

Hack, W., C. Candoli, and J. Roy. 1995. *School Business Administration*. 5th ed. Needham Heights, MA: Allyn & Bacon.

Hammer, M., and J. Champy. 1993. *Reengineering the Corporation*. New York: Harper Collins, p. 32.

Hax, A., and N. Majluf. 1991. *The Strategy Process and Concept—A Pragmatic Approach*. Englewood Cliffs, NJ: Prentice-Hall.

Hencley, S. P,. and J. R. Yates. 1974. *Futurism in Education*. Berkeley, CA: McCutchen Publishing Corporation, p. 12–26.

Imai, M. 1986. *KAIZEN*. New York: Random House Business Division, p. 3, 25.

Kendall, G. 1998. *Securing the Future: Strategies for Exponential Growth Using the Theory of Constraints*. Boca Raton, FL: St. Lucie Press.

Makridakis, S. 1990. *Forecasting, Planning, and Strategy for the 21st Century*. New York: The Free Press.

Marrus, S. 1984. *Building the Strategic Plan*. New York: John Wiley & Sons, p. 4.

MBNQA. 1995. *Midstate University Case Study*. Gaithersburg, MD: National Institute of Standards and Technology, p. 1.

Millett, S. M., and E. J. Honton. 1991. *A Manager's Guide to Technology Forecasting and Strategy Analysis Methods*. Columbus, OH: Battle Press, p. 2.

Norris, D., and N. Poulton. 1991. *A Guide for New Planners*. Ann Arbor, MI: The Society for College and University Planning, p. 9–11.

Owens, R. 1994. *Organizational Behavior in Education*. 5th ed. Needham Heights, MA: Allyn & Bacon.

Rothwell, W., and H. C. Kazanas. 1994. *Planning and Managing Human Resources*. Amherst, MA: HRD Press, p. 1–2.

Scherkenbach, W. 1990. *The Deming Route to Quality and Productivity*. Rockville, MD: Mercury Press, p. 13.

Senge, P. 1990. *The Fifth Discipline*. New York: Currency and Doubleday, p. 12.

Shipley, J. 1993. *Total Quality Schooling: A Plan to Empower a Community*. Largo, FL: Pinellas County School District, The Quality Academy.

Wheelwright, S. C., and S. Makridakis. 1985. *Forecasting Methods for Management*. New York: John Wiley & Sons, p. 10–19.

Chapter 3

Futuring Tools and their Use

"The trouble with the future is that it usually arrives before we're ready for it."

—Arnold H. Glasow

Futuring Tools for Strategic Quality Planning in Education provides a set of seven practical tools that allow organizations and teams to conduct activities that produce methods for looking into the future of an organization. This chapter provides detailed explanations of what the tools are, how they are related, and how they are used. The chapter also explains the organization of the tools in chapters 4 through 10.

Tool Classification

There are many "toolkits" on the market, such as GOAL/QPC's *The Memory Jogger* and *The Memory Jogger II*, Glen Hoffherr's *The Toolbook: Decision Making & Planning for Optimum Results*, the *Total Quality Transformation* tools by QIP/PQ Systems, Field's *Total Quality for Schools*, the *Koalaty Kid Tool Kit*, and a number of tool descriptions from industry, including IBM and AT&T corporations. See references for others. However, there are few resources that can be used by managers and leaders to learn simple techniques to help them plan for the future. Figure 3-1 identifies several of the more commonly used tools that have assisted managers in planning, decision making, predicting, and managing long-term and daily tasks.

Classification	Name of Tools
Quality Improvement Tools	Cause and Effect Diagram, Pareto Diagram, Line Chart, Flow Diagram, Check Sheet, Histogram, and Control Diagram
Management and Planning Tools	Affinity Diagram, Interrelationship Digraph, Tree Diagram, Prioritization Matrix, Matrix Diagram, Process Decision Program Chart, and Activity Network Chart
And now . . . Futuring Tools	Trend Extrapolation, Delphi Technique, Morphological Analysis, Crawford Slip Method, Scenario Planning, Cross-Impact Analysis, and Futuring Tree

Figure 3-1. Classification of tools.

Tool Selection Criteria

The need to plan for the future is more evident now than ever before. The continuous and dynamic rate of change in our society and schools demands that we plan for the future, both short-range and long-range. In the midst of all the turmoil, is there an easier way to get planning done? The authors reviewed many documents and tested several planning and decision-making tools to see which were best suited for the busy manager.

The *quality improvement tools* are designed to analyze current problems and processes to find variation and solutions for improvement. The *management and planning tools* focus more broadly on the development and analysis of ideas and processes. Although these tools employ analytical procedures that may impact an organization's future, they are predominantly present-oriented.

The authors examined myriad lists of tools, "tool kits," "tool boxes," and the like. Those tools that are dedicated to developing an organization's vision and strategic quality future were separated and reviewed. Two notable tools reviewed were Marvin Weisbord's *Future Search* and Joel Barker's *Implications Wheel*.

Future Search is a strategic planning process wherein a sizable group of stakeholders meet to create an agreed-upon strategic plan framework for an organization that can be committed to action. The process focuses on resolving conflicts, generating commitment to common goals, and developing creative strategies that can be transformed into action by the organization. The basic principle is to involve the "whole system" to work from a global perspective to create the strategic plan. The "whole system" represents a cross section of stakeholders such as management, employees, customers, suppliers, regulators, government, and community members. The process is conducted through a "future search conference." (See Weisbord 1995.)

Joel Barker's *Implications Wheel* is a strategic exploration and decision-enhancing process that helps organizations to explore the implications of trends, issues, policies, innovations, and events. Similar to the Trend Extrapolation tool, the wheel allows users to explore and extend linear trends and the like, and records both negative and positive implications that can influence the organization's future. These "ripples of change" provide information on how the organization may be impacted in the short- and long-term future. The process includes a scoring system that assists the organization in determining the desirability and likelihood of the implications, as well as providing some understanding of the interrelationships between specific implications. This process seems to parallel the external and internal scanning described earlier, which imposes limitations on its use as a futuring tool as defined by the authors (Barker 1994).

Four criteria were used in the selection of the seven tools described in this book. They are simplicity, functionality, time-testedness, and interconnectivity.

1. Simplicity. Keeping in mind the harried daily life of the educational manager, the search was made for tools that were relatively easy to use with a minimal amount of training. They were also selected to be used by individuals and teams without the use of high-powered computer processes.

2. Functionality. Whatever the tool, if it does not fulfill the function it was intended for, it will be useless to the manager. The seven futuring tools are practical in every sense of the word. In the description of each tool is an explanation of how the tool can be used and for what purpose.

3. Time-Testedness. No new planning tools are developed in *Futuring Tools*. The authors looked for tools that have been used in a number of situations with success and were time-tested. In the cases where examples were limited, the intent was to identify a tool that has been in use for a number of years and is still in the current literature. An example of this is the Morphological Analysis. While examples are scarce, its creativity and continued citation in forecasting literature identify it as a potentially useful tool.

4. Interconnectivity. The tools were selected to work dynamically with each other. While they can be used in many situations alone, their usefulness is enhanced when used in pairs or triads. The section in this chapter on the dynamic relationship among the futuring tools will demonstrate this interrelatedness.

The Seven Futuring Tools

Trend Extrapolation
Delphi Technique
Morphological Analysis
Crawford Slip Method
Scenario Planning
Cross-Impact Analysis
Futuring Tree

Each futuring tool is distinguishable from the others by its purpose and outcome. Additionally, the model, structure, or look of each tool is unique. To assist in remembering these tools, icons were developed for each tool. These icons provide a graphic representation of the tool and will be repeated throughout the book.

The icons and a brief explanation provide an introduction to each tool.

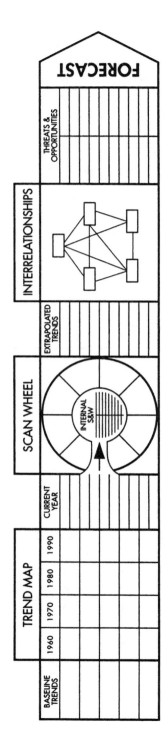

Figure 3-2. Trend Extrapolation model. This tool identifies, collects, and analyzes trend patterns of the past and present, their extrapolation, and probable impact on the future of an organization.

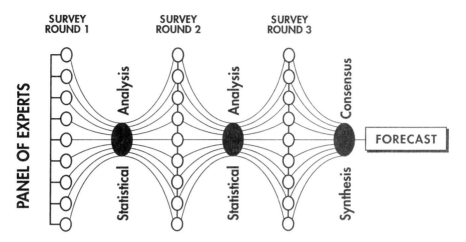

Figure 3-3. Delphi Technique model. This tool is a process for extracting expert intuitive expectations of alternative possible futures through repeated surveys and analysis.

Morphological Box

$P_{1.0}$	$E_{1.1}$,	$E_{1.2}$,	$E_{1.3}$,	$E_{1.4}$,	$E_{1.5}$
$P_{2.0}$	$E_{2.1}$,	$E_{2.2}$,	$E_{2.3}$,	$E_{2.4}$	$E_{2.5}$
$P_{3.0}$	$E_{3.1}$,	$E_{3.2}$,	$E_{3.3}$		
$P_{4.0}$	$E_{4.1}$,	$E_{4.2}$,	$E_{4.3}$,	$E_{4.4}$	
$P_{5.0}$	$E_{5.1}$,	$E_{5.2}$,	$E_{5.3}$,	$E_{5.4}$	
$P_{6.0}$	$E_{6.1}$,	$E_{6.2}$,	$E_{6.3}$		
$P_{7.0}$	$E_{7.1}$,	$E_{7.2}$,	$E_{7.3}$		
$P_{8.0}$	$E_{8.1}$,	$E_{8.2}$,	$E_{8.3}$,	$E_{8.4}$,	$E_{8.5}$
$P_{9.0}$	$E_{9.1}$,	$E_{9.2}$,	$E_{9.3}$,	$E_{9.4}$	
$P_{10.0}$	$E_{10.1}$,	$E_{10.2}$,	$E_{10.3}$		

Figure 3-4. Morphological Analysis model. This tool is a method for producing numerous creative solutions to a problem by discovering and analyzing the form, structure, and interrelationships among phenomena in an unprejudiced context and then extrapolating multiple solutions.

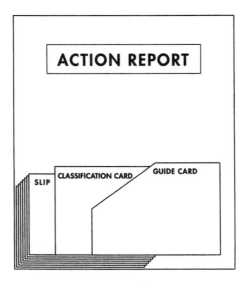

Figure 3-5. Crawford Slip Method model. This tool is a technique for gathering and organizing a large number of ideas that have been brainstormed independently, simultaneously, anonymously, and rapidly in a think-tank environment.

Write short stories of what might happen.

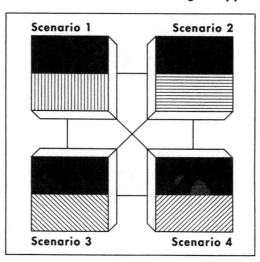

Figure 3-6. Scenario Planning model. This tool is a process for developing stories or likely series of events that provide alternative futures, with a focus on predetermined and uncertain environments, for the purpose of decision making.

EVENT MATRIX

The effect on this event is...

If this event occurs —	E1	E2	E3	E4	E5
E1	■				
E2		■			
E3			■		
E4				■	
E5					■

Figure 3-7. Cross-Impact Analysis model. This tool depicts the interdependence that occurs among selected future events by employing probability to communicate the likelihood that certain events will exert influence on or be influenced by other events and to determine the cumulative impact.

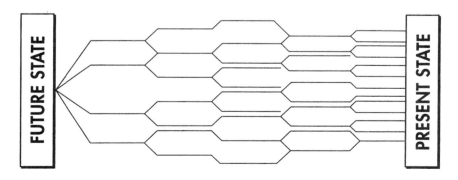

Figure 3-8. Futuring Tree model. This tool starts with a future goal and works backwards through a network of alternative pathways to connect the organization's future with its present.

The Interrelationships among the Tools

For a set of tools to be useful they have to both stand alone and be interactive. Figure 3-9 depicts the interactivity among the seven futuring tools. The first five tools—Trend Extrapolation, Delphi Technique, Morphological Analysis, Crawford Slip Method, and Scenario Planning—are usually the starting place for any future planning. One or several of the tools can be used in this phase of the planning. Following the preliminary planning, the information from this first phase goes to the second phase, or Cross-Impact Analysis. The final phase of the process is the use of the Futuring Tree. While the process just described is a model for using the tools, these tools can also be used independently.

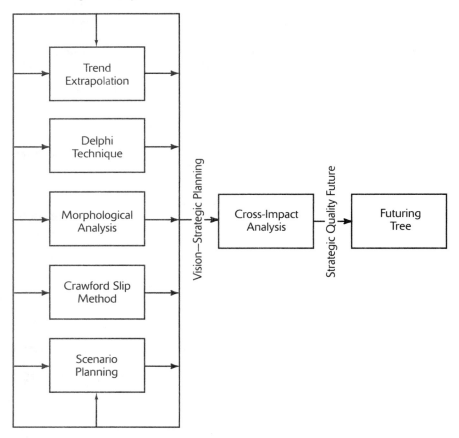

Figure 3-9. The futuring tools interrelationship.

Organization of the Tools Chapters

There are seven tools explained in detail in chapters 4 through 10. Each tool has its own chapter with discussion and is organized in response to the seven questions:

1. What is its *purpose*? This section provides an explanation of the background and purpose of the tool.

2. What is its *definition*? This section provides definitions from research and develops an operational definition for users of the futuring tools.

3. What are its *operational characteristics*? This section provides a list of characteristics of each tool, to enable the user to better understand each tool's uses and limitations.

4. What is its *structure*? This section presents a graphic model and explains what the technique or tool looks like when applied in an actual situation.

5. What are *examples of its use*? This section provides actual and simulated examples of uses of the tool.

6. What is its *process*? This section provides a step-by-step procedure for how the tool is developed.

7. What are *variations of this tool*? When appropriate, this section provides a discussion of various alternative ways the tool can be used. Response to this question will also identify other tools that produce similar results.

References

Barker, J. 1994. *Implications Wheel*. A video by Aurora Pictures, Minneapolis, MN 55406-9861.

Brassard, M. 1988. *The Memory Jogger*. Methuen, MA: GOAL/QPC.

———. 1995. *The Memory Jogger II*. Methuen, MA: GOAL/QPC.

———. 1988. *The Memory Jogger Plus + Featuring the Seven Management and Planning Tools*. Methuen, MA: GOAL/QPC.

Collett, C., *et al*. 1992. *Making Daily Management Work*. Methuen, MA: GOAL/QPC.

Cowley, M., and E. Domb. 1997. *Beyond Strategic Vision*. Methuen, MA: GOAL/QPC.

Hoffherr, G. D. 1993. *The Toolbook: Decision Making & Planning for Optimum Results*. Windham, NH: Markon.

King, B. 1989. *Hoshin Planning: The Developmental Approach*. Methuen, MA: GOAL/QPC.

Norton, M. S., L. D. Webb, L. Dlugosh, and W. Sybouts. 1996. *The School Superintendency: New Responsibilities, New Leadership*. Needham Heights, MA: Allyn & Bacon.

Ozeki, K., and T. Asaka. 1990. *Handbook of Quality Tools: The Japanese Approach*. Cambridge: Productivity Press.

Weisbord, M., and S. Janoff. 1995. *Future Search: An Action Guide to Finding Common Ground in Organizations and Communities*. San Francisco: Berrett-Koehler.

Chapter 4

Trend Extrapolation

"Getting to the future is a process of successive approximation."

—Hamel and Prahalad

Trend Extrapolation is a relatively simple tool that may be used to fore-cast an organization's strategic future. The selection and use of this tool is based upon the supposition that those factors that have produced trends or organizational changes in the past are constant and will continue to influence the future. This tool provides a reasonably clear picture of where the organization is headed and what might be done about it, particularly in the near future.

What Is Its Purpose?

The purpose of this tool is to ascertain to what extent the future of an organization might be influenced by certain trends. Trends appear at different levels such as the local, state, national, and global levels. Naisbitt and Aburdene (1990) talk about megatrends in their book *Megatrends 2000*. These global trends will likely impact all organizations to some degree, since they are broad extrapolated statements of significant trend patterns at a global level. The myriad trends at the local, state, and national levels will affect organizations differently or not at all. The important thing is to be sure that the trends selected for analysis and extrapolation are in fact those trends most likely to influence the organization's future.

What Is Its Definition?

Trend Extrapolation may be defined as the identification, collection, and analysis of trend patterns of the past and present, their extrapolation, and their probable impact on the future of an organization.

What Are Its Operational Characteristics?

Trend Extrapolation has several operational characteristics that profile its usefulness and assist planning teams in selecting the most appropriate tool for strategic quality planning. Following is a description of the most important characteristics:

1. Easy to use. Because the tool has been widely used in the past, the procedure is well known and easily understood by educators at all levels. Identifying and extrapolating trends is not a new idea, so it takes little time to orient a planning team in how to use the tool. The process is a logical one; it begins with the selection of baseline trends, recalls their history of influence, summarizes where they are currently, and extrapolates likely changes in the future.

2. Requires few resources. Trends are rather easy to identify and document. The search and confirmation of trends may be conducted in a library or workshop environment where representatives from key areas of the organization input their recollection and experience with the trends being considered. Printed descriptions of trends from newspapers, magazines, focused books, and futurists' prognostications are readily available.

3. Results are strengthened through the environmental scans. Targeting the search for influences on internal and external trends through environmental scanning is an important step in providing objectivity to the process. Researching and collecting data on these influences and their impact provides the team with consistent information from which a more accurate forecast can be made.

4. Provides further focus on cause/effect relationships among trends. Examination of relationships among the trends offers a more thorough understanding of the trend characteristics. This procedure is

a reinforcing effort to provide a more systematic process for developing a forecast or vision for an organization.

What Is Its Structure?

Trend Extrapolation is a process that involves determining baseline trends that occur within the organization, tracking their progress as well as the impact of other trends to the present, conducting internal and external environmental scans, analyzing trend patterns, discovering internal strengths and weaknesses as well as external threats and opportunities, extrapolating key trends, analyzing their causal relationships, and creating a forecast. The model in Figure 4-1 displays the Trend Extrapolation process for forecasting an organization's strategic future.

What Are Examples of Its Use?

Trend Extrapolation has been used for decades to analyze where organizations are headed. It is widely used in industry, health care, government, and education. Examining trends has been the foundation for educational planning for many decades and is still commonly used today. Prior to the arrival of strategic planning, long-range and annual plans were predominantly trend-based. This, combined with the intuitive abilities of leaders, was the forerunner of attempts to envision a future for education. One can easily see the process at work today. Originally, extrapolating the trends was the problem. Attempts to scan the internal and external environments for influence were usually made at committee meetings or brief workshops, where ideas were simply brainstormed at the moment. There was little systemic or systematic process involved.

More recently, as the rigor of strategic planning has been employed, the trend extrapolation process has become more meaningful and accurate. The model in this chapter strengthens the research and database ingredient required for accurate forecasting.

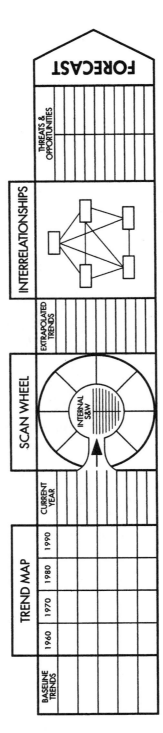

Figure 4-1. Trend Extrapolation model.

What Is Its Process?

The Trend Extrapolation process requires several steps. It is important that each step be completed as objectively as possible, since each builds upon the results of the prior step. A second concern is to ensure that the appropriate trends are selected for extrapolation. These become critical success factors in the model. The trends selected must be allowed a sufficient time period for observation and analysis. For example, some trends may be *seasonal* and increase or decrease during certain seasons of the year. Another caution in trend analysis is the *cyclic* characteristic whereby trends seem to recycle over a given period of months or years. Examples of this can be seen in clothing fashions such as wide ties, jacket lapels, pleated skirts, shoes, and clothing fabrics. Color choice has become cyclic on automobiles as well as clothing. One can often estimate the year of manufacture of a vehicle by the color combinations used.

A third caution for analysts is the *trendshock* phenomenon. This causes trends to change rapidly in different directions. Often new trends are created or old trends destroyed during this phenomenon. Trendshock has been caused by such events as the launching of the Russian Sputnik, the death of President John F. Kennedy, the recent stock market crash on Wall Street, the Desert Storm war, political elections, and the like.

An explanation of the steps in conducting a Trend Extrapolation follows.

Trend Extrapolation

Step 1:	Select the Appropriate Team
Step 2:	Identify Baseline Trends
Step 3:	Complete a Trendmap of the Organization
Step 4:	Conduct Environmental Scans
Step 5:	Extrapolate Trends
Step 6:	Analyze Cause-Effect Relationships
Step 7:	Determine Future Threats and Opportunities
Step 8:	Prepare the Forecast

Figure 4.2. Steps in developing a Trend Extrapolation.

Step 1: Select the Appropriate Team

School

The future planning team must have representation from key function areas of the organization. Whether it is a school, district, or college, the team size may range from 12 to approximately 18 members, depending upon the size of the organization. In addition to representation from all functions of the organization, all levels of personnel, parents, community leaders, industry, students, and stakeholders should be included.

Step 2: Identify Baseline Trends

Once the strategic planning team has been organized and charged, the first consideration is to decide which trends or trend patterns they should analyze. Organizations are bombarded with myriad trends, requiring the team to select those most crucial to the continued success of the organization. These are called *baseline trends*, since they become the focus of the extrapolation process. Examples of trends that can be used for baselining are shown in Figure 4-3.

Different organizations will prefer variations in this list based upon their history, goals, and possible future.

Step 3: Complete a Trendmap of the Organization

A *trendmap* tells a story about the organization and allows participants to observe patterns in trends that have impacted the recent history of the

1. Leadership philosophy	7. Applications of technology
2. Key innovations and ideas	8. Curriculum
3. Finance/accounting procedures	9. Employee satisfaction
4. Community involvement and activities	10. Professional development
5. Buildings, grounds, and facilities	11. Employee demographics
6. State and national requirements	12. Resource procurement

Figure 4-3. Common baseline trends.

Baseline Trends	1960	1970	1980	1990	Current year
1.					
2.					
3.					
4.					
5.					
6.					

Figure 4-4. Sample trendmap of organization.

organization. The selection and recording of these trends represents a shared base of information about the organization. The activity is focused around the baseline trends. Figure 4-4 shows an example of a trendmap that uses selected baseline trends noted earlier.

To begin the trendmap, make a large grid similar to Figure 4-4 and post it on a flat wall. The grid should be approximately 4 feet by 6 feet in size. The trendmap usually goes back four decades (1990, 1980, 1970, 1960) and adds a column for Current Year Trends on the extreme right. A column for baseline trends that satisfy the criteria described in Step 2 is attached to the far left. Team members brainstorm to recall events, changes, new ideas, and the like in each of the baseline trend areas over the time periods shown on the trendmap. These events, changes, ideas, innovations, and activities are written on Post-it slips and placed appropriately on the grid. Following this, sketches or icons may be added or substituted to clarify the historical influences. Finally, trends occurring in the current year are added in the column at the right.

The team now analyzes the trendmap for patterns, which are identified and noted in the current year trend column as well.

Step 4: Conduct Environmental Scans

Environmental scans produce information on trends that are internal and external to the organization. An internal scan may be obtained from the information in the Current Year Trends column, which reveals internal trends and patterns that are currently influencing the organization. From this analysis, internal strengths and weaknesses of the organization may be ascertained. They are listed in the center portion of the Scan Wheel shown in Figure 4-5.

A review of trends external to the organization is very important to recognizing new patterns and how they might affect the organization's future. This is accomplished through the external environmental scan procedure. The team identifies categories of trends that are or may become relevant to the organization in the future. These categories are posted around the perimeter of the Scan Wheel. Several sources of information are available for external scanning, including government reports, database depository

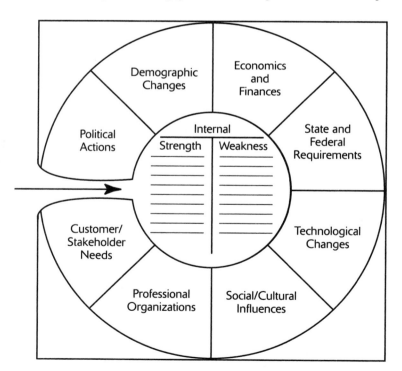

Figure 4-5. The Scan Wheel, showing the external environment scan criteria and the internal strengths and weaknesses.

Trend Category	
Current Trends	Projected Changes*

*Show sources of information and data.

Figure 4-6. Trend identification worksheet.

centers, library reference collections, professional organizations, agency research, and publications by futurists.

The team should subdivide responsibilities for collecting data on each of the categories selected. It is important that the external trend research be done rigorously rather than relying on brainstorming to identify the trends. A Trend Identification Worksheet, shown in Figure 4-6, will assist team members in selecting targeted trends and recording research-based information that implies or describes projected changes or new trends in each category.

During the search for external trends, you might look for best-in-class practices in organizations similar to yours. It is not uncommon to find other organizations that have significantly improved one or more practices toward achieving best-in-class performance. If this opportunity exists, a benchmarking process should be established between the organizations; this may provide valuable information that can impact positively on your organization's future.

Step 5: Extrapolate Trends

Extrapolation is a procedure for inferring that which is unknown from that which is known (Webster 1989). Step 5 involves just that. The team must now study the trend data collected from the internal and external scans and extrapolate the targeted trends five to ten years into the future. The extrapolations are listed in random order on a flip chart or wall chart positioned as shown in the model in Figure 4-1. Many of the extrapolations may be developed directly from the extensions of projected changes in trends listed on the Trend Identification Worksheet. See Figure 4-6.

Extrapolation statements should be brief and succinct. They should describe the trend as it might appear five to ten years from now. Wording is important. Once the list is complete, team members should reach consensus with the list.

Step 6: Analyze Cause-Effect Relationships

Following consensus on the list of extrapolated trends, the next step is to analyze these trends for direct cause-effect relationships. This is done to discover which of the trends are "drivers" and which are "driven." These cause-effect relationships are valuable to the team as they begin to think about the forecast this process will produce.

The relationships are revealed by use of the Interrelationship Digraph, which uses a series of arrows to show which trends affect which of the other trends. The procedure may be quantified by counting the number of arrows coming into each trend box and the number going out from each box. See Figure 4-7 for a sample cause-effect analysis of extrapolated trends.

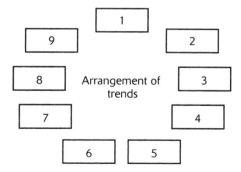

Figure 4-7. Cause-effect relationships among the extrapolated trends.

Nine extrapolated trends are displayed in Figure 4-7. The analysis begins by asking the question, Does trend 1 affect trend 2? If yes, an arrow is drawn from block 1 to block 2. If the answer is no, no arrows are drawn. The team proceeds by asking whether trend 1 affects trend 3. This procedure continues in a clockwise direction examining 1 and 4, 1 and 5, 1 and 6 and so on. Arrows are drawn where appropriate. The next round begins with trend 2 and examines the cause-effect relationships between 2 and 1, 2 and 3, 2 and 4, and so on until all nine trends have been analyzed. Scoring is done by counting the number of arrows going outward from each trend box and recording the number. O/4, for instance, means there are four arrows going out. Arrows coming into each box are also counted and recorded. I/2 indicates there are two arrows coming into the box. Each of the trend boxes shows its score.

Those trends with the highest "out" scores are considered drivers and create influential relationships with others. These are important since they will likely impact most on the organization's future. Those trends with high "in" scores are more dependent and less influential than the drivers.

Step 7: Determine Future Threats and Opportunities

A review of the extrapolated trends and their cause-effect analysis provides the team with information that can reveal threats or opportunities related to the organization's future. Threats are described as forces within these extrapolated trends that could have a negative effect on the achievement of the organization's strategic future. Opportunities, however, offer the organization options and positive reinforcement in the pursuit of the vision and strategic planning.

Step 8: Prepare the Forecast

The final step in this process is to study the results produced so far by the team and prepare a forecast for the organization. This forecast is written in narrative form and is used in drafting a vision of what the organization may be like five to ten years from now. With the information gained from this process, the team can go beyond the vision and propose strategic and tactical plans that will guide the organization in achieving its strategic future.

The results obtained from Trend Extrapolation represent a systematic process for tracking prior trends and extrapolating key trends in the context of information garnered from the environmental scans. The internal consistency of the process is achieved through tracking key trends and trend patterns.

The integrity of the process is maintained by the consensus on baseline trends and extrapolations, research-based information produced by the environmental scans, and the cause-effect relationship analysis. These procedures tend to minimize subjective decision making, thereby giving more credibility to the resulting forecast.

Another point to consider is that the forecast may not reflect the organization's preferred future. It more likely represents the probable future. If this is unsatisfactory to the organization, then an articulated tactical plan must be put into place to influence the extrapolated trends.

What Are Variations of this Tool?

One variation of this tool is to identify key baseline trends through consensus and extrapolate those trends individually using an Extrapolation Map. In this process, each trend is posted in a center circle and extrapolated outward in different directions according to the perceived changes. This bypasses the trendmap. See Figure 4-8.

The environmental scans are then complete. A list is composed of those scan trends most likely to influence the future of the organization. These scan trends are placed on the Interrelationship Digraph along with the

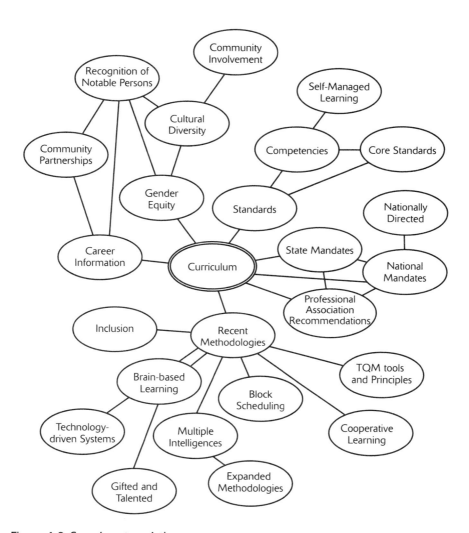

Figure 4-8. Sample extrapolation map.

extrapolated trends and analyzed for cause-effect relationships. From this, a list of threats and opportunities can be developed, as before, that forms the basis for drafting a forecast.

References

Armstrong, J. S. 1985. *Long-Range Forecasting: From Crystal Ball to Computer.* 2d ed. New York: John Wiley & Sons.

Barker, J. A. 1985. *Discovering the Future: The Business of Paradigms*. St. Paul, MN: ILI Press.

Brassard, M. 1989. *The Memory Jogger Plus*. Methuen, MA: GOAL/QPC.

Cetron, M., and M. Gayle. 1991. *Educational Renaissance: Our Schools at the Turn of the 21st Century*. New York: St. Martins Press.

Chandler, R. 1992. *Racing Towards 2001: The Forces Shaping America's Religious Future*. Grand Rapids, MI: Zondervan Publishing House.

Fowles, J. 1978. *Handbook of Futures Research*. Westport, CT: Greenwood Press.

Martino, J. 1983. *Technological Forecasting for Decision Making*. 2d ed. New York: North Holland Publishers, p. 78.

Naisbitt, J., and P. Aberdene. 1990. *Megatrends 2000*. New York: William Morrow and Company.

Nanus, B. 1992. *Visionary Leadership*. San Francisco: Jossey-Bass Publishers.

Sergiovanni, T. 1995. *The Principalship: A Reflective Practice Perspective*. 3d ed. Needham Heights, MA: Allyn & Bacon.

Chapter 5

Delphi Technique

Planners have long realized that the answers to their problems cannot be found through the use of an oracle. In ancient Greece, however, this was not the case. One of the most acclaimed oracles of ancient times was at Delphi, atop Mount Parnassus. Here worshipers came from all over Greece to search for the wisdom they needed. Today, planners must look not to an oracle, but rather to experts, for their opinions in developing plans for the future. If experts always agreed on the solutions to problems, the solutions would be easier to implement. In reality, however, this rarely happens. The Delphi Technique offers a way to bring those expert opinions together.

What Is Its Purpose?

The Delphi Technique, or as it is often called, the "Jury of Executive Opinion" method, is a well-used futuring tool that is useful in getting issues focused by surveying experts in a field rather than the general population. The intent of the process is to bring together people who have expert knowledge about a subject, for they are the people most likely to know, or at least be in a position to know, the answers. The experts respond to survey questions on a topic under study. The results of the survey are then gathered and analyzed to get a general opinion of the pool of experts. Usually, many experts in a particular field are used in this process.

What Is Its Definition?

Joel Kurtzman defines the Delphi Technique as "a highly structured method for polling experts on their considered opinions about some aspect of the future. It attempts to get a consensus of expert opinion on the issue under consideration" (1984). The Delphi Technique, Delphi Method, or simply Delphi, was developed by mathematician Olaf Helmer while working with the Rand Corporation in California. The Rand Corporation developed this process in order to "obtain the most reliable consensus of opinions of a group of experts by a series of intensive questionnaires interspersed with controlled opinion feedback" (Dakley and Helmer 1963). It is one of the most popular futuring tools for assessing future technology innovations, policy impact, and social change. It is valuable for creating alternative futures and works well with Cross-Impact Analysis in developing the main issue or theme.

The Delphi Technique, then, is defined as a multi-step systematic process for extracting expert intuitive expectations (forecasts) of alternate possible futures. It is only as valid as the group of experts selected for the expert team. This tool is useful for obtaining estimates or judgments of alternative futures, the expected time frame for events, expected breakthroughs, and future opportunities, as well as a value judgment as to whether an event should be enhanced or inhibited. This technique is a consensus technique and has been used extensively for technological forecasting.

What Are Its Operational Characteristics?

The Delphi Technique provides the planner with several distinguishing operational characteristics.

1. Involves experts in the field. An important characteristic of the Delphi is the ability to gather the opinion of experts without the necessity of bringing them together. This can save time and money. A modification of the technique, however, allows for experts gathering together in a retreat-like setting.

2. Solves complex problems. The Delphi has a reputation for solving complex problems through the survey and analysis process. Through each round of questioning, the statements begin to develop until the final product is produced.

3. Is accurate. Studies have shown that the Delphi correlates significantly with actual trend assessment. The repetitiveness of the questions and their continued analysis lends high reliability.

4. Respects anonymity. Most Delphi processes respect the anonymity of the participants, thus allowing respondents to voice their true opinions without any justification. In the latter stages of the process, the names of the respondents are often released, although their responses are not.

What Is Its Structure?

The Delphi Technique model in Figure 5-1 provides a graphic representation of the Delphi Technique. It depicts a series of nine experts (represented by small circles) being brought together to provide answers and analysis to

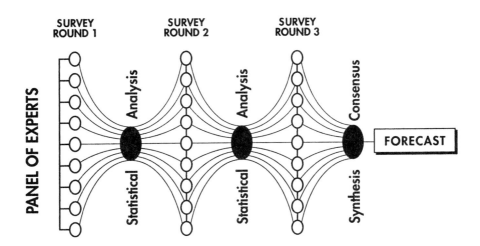

Figure 5-1. Delphi Technique model.

a situation (represented by the black oval). This analysis generates revised questions that are answered by the experts and analyzed again. The survey is once again re-administered and re-analyzed. The final product is displayed in the box on the right.

What Are Examples of Its Use?

An example of a Delphi Technique survey was conducted recently in a local public school to obtain opinions about future facility needs (Cherry Hill Public Schools 1991). After generating a survey on the facilities topic with a local team, the survey was sent to a panel of experts asking for their input and additional issues that may have been overlooked. The format, along with several questions from that survey, are shown in Figure 5-2. The experts were asked to respond to each statement in two ways. First, for each statement, the experts were asked to "pick a year between now and 2010" for

Statement	Pick a Year between Now and 2010 for which the Statement has a 50% Probability of Reoccurrence	Probability of Occurrence by 2000
1. Schools will equip each student with his/her own instrument of technology, such as interactive sound and video, that will provide access to world information.		
2. Schools will provide flexible interior settings for varied instructional techniques and administrative purposes.		
3. To provide 24-hour, year-round use of buildings, schools will provide proper "conditioning" of the environment.		

Figure 5-2. Sample questions on school Delphi Technique survey. (Courtesy of Cherry Hill Schools, NJ.)

Statement (Listed in order)	Mean Year Selected Between Now and 2010 that Has 50% Probability of Occurrence	Mean Percent Indicating Probability of Occur-rence by 2000
6. Parents and teachers will exercise increased involvement in school management and curriculum.	1998	75.90
8. Schools will provide access to computerized reference informa-tion for school and home use.	2000	67.64
11. Based on the needs of the family and each child, the school com-munity will create learning and developmental experiences in the early childhood years.	2000	65.85
13. Schools will provide facilities for day care, organized recreation, senior citizen centers, and other community needs.	1999	58.40

Figure 5-3. Sample results of the Delphi Technique survey. (Courtesy of Cherry Hill Schools, NJ.)

which the statement "has a 50 percent probability of occurrence." Second, in regard to the statement, the experts were asked for a "probability of occur-rence by 2000."

After tallying the results and sending out the survey additional times, the results were presented in a report addressed to the school district and com-munity. A sample of the results is shown in Figure 5-3. The school district used this information to develop long-range facility plans.

What Is Its Process?

The steps shown in Figure 5-4 are used in implementing the Delphi Technique.

Delphi Technique

Step 1:	Select a Team
Step 2:	Identify the Main Issue
Step 3:	Develop a Questionnaire
Step 4:	Select a Panel of Experts
Step 5:	First-Round Survey and Tally
Step 6:	Second-Round Survey and Tally
Step 7:	Third-Round Survey and Tally
Step 8:	Interpret the Results

Figure 5-4. Steps in conducting the Delphi Technique.

Step 1: Select a Team

It is important that the development of the questions or statements in the Delphi Technique survey be the responsibility both of people who are part of the organization, and of people outside the organization who are major stakeholders or customers. This includes the people in the organization with the knowledge, interest, and enthusiasm to work for a better organization. In this way, employees can be part of the process and feel ownership of the decisions and relationships that may be developed. Once the team is formed, they can proceed to Step 2.

Step 2: Identify the Main Issue

The next step in the process is for the team to identify the main issue, focus, or theme of the Delphi Technique survey process, if the team is empowered to do this. Otherwise, the main issue may be given to the team by the superintendent, board, or other directing agency. Keep in mind that this process is designed to clarify strategic decisions that will be made by the organization; that is, to answer the question, What is the best decision we need to make based on the results of our survey? The main issue can be stated in broad

How can we develop a vision for our school district?
When will the price of gold stabilize?
When will technology be fully implemented?
What will be the characteristics of standard-setting organizations in 2020?
What will the impact of new media on the conventional consumer magazine industry be?
What will be the impact of emerging technologies?

Figure 5-5. Examples of Delphi Technique statements or questions.

terms, such as, "How can we gather information about the use of technology in our school district in the next ten years?" or as specific as "How should we develop our in-school suspension program for the future?" Defining a good main issue is important to the process. It will provide the motivation for the team and identify the process as worthwhile. Several examples of main issues identified in Delphi Technique surveys are listed in Figure 5-5.

The Delphi Technique is a good tool to use when trying to produce a generic forecast, for instance when asking How can we develop a vision for our department?

Step 3: Develop a Questionnaire

Once the focus is determined, a questionnaire is developed. This can be accomplished through focus groups or by the Delphi team selected in Step 1. The details for the survey questions need to be developed based on the goals and requirements of the selected focus or theme.

The construction of the survey can take on varied forms. The respondent can be asked to check off given responses, such as in Figure 5-6, where the responses are asked for in years. Or the results can be to fill in a response, such as in Figure 5-7. The response can be in a 5-point Likert scale that ranges from very important (5) to not important (1). Another option allows for a series of possible responses in which the respondent selects a response or prioritizes the responses.

Technological Innovation	2000	2004	2008	2012	2016	2020 and beyond
Computers required for every student	(2000)					
Access to the Internet for every student			(2008)			
Year-round schools		(2004)				
Self-managed schools			(2008)			

Figure 5-6. Example of Delphi Technique survey responding to the use of technological innovations in universities, where respondent checks the appropriate date.

Step 4: Select a Panel of Experts

The panel of experts is selected from people knowledgeable in the field related to the question or area under investigation. This is one of the most important steps in the process and sets the Delphi Technique apart from a standard survey or interview technique. Normally the panel of experts is spread throughout the state or nation, so the panel rarely comes together. There are occasions, however, when panels congregate to provide a variation to the reg-

Technological Innovation	Fill in Date
Computers required for every student	2000
Access to the Internet for every student	2008
Interactive media home instruction	2012
Year-round schools	2004
Self-managed schools	2008

Figure 5-7. Example of Delphi Technique survey responding to the use of technological innovations in universities where dates are to be entered by the respondent.

ular Delphi Technique. With the advancements in the Internet, Delphi questionnaires are being placed on line via the World Wide Web.[1] Respondents are providing voluntary input while providing a biography of their relative expertise. The survey manager weighs the level of expertise. This method has its advantages and disadvantages, but more importantly, demonstrates the potential of on-line surveying for implementing a future tool.

The number of respondents on the panel can vary from ten to several hundred. Fifty or one hundred is usually satisfactory depending on responses. There is no consensus on what constitutes a "best" panel. The number of people on a panel has varied greatly with successful results. Once the panel is chosen, an introductory letter and the questionnaire is sent.

Step 5: First-Round Survey and Tally

The first-round survey is sent to the panel of experts with instructions. Normally the names of the other panel members are not revealed at this time. This is also the time to ask the experts for their feedback on the questions being asked. The Delphi Technique team can use this information to revise the survey. If too many corrections are made, it might call for an additional round. Usually this request for additional information is asked in the first round and not in subsequent rounds.

The responses to the survey are tallied and placed in graphical form for ease in review for the next round. An example is shown in Figure 5-8.

Technological Innovation	2000	2004	2008	2012	2016	2020 and beyond
Computers required for every student	43	14	3			
Access to the Internet for every student	10	38	12			

Figure 5-8. Tallied results from the first round of 60 participants.

---

[1]George Washington University, School of Business and Public Management conducted a 1996 Delphi Survey on Emerging Issues over the Internet. Responses were requested with the survey, along with a biography to determine how expert the respondent was.

Technological Innovation	2000	2004	2008	2012	2016	2020 and beyond
Computers required for every student	45	12	3			
Access to the Internet for every student	9	46	5			

Figure 5-9. Tallied results from the second round of 60 participants.

Step 6: Second-Round Survey and Tally

A revised questionnaire is sent to the panel along with the results of the first round. The names of the panel members may also be included. Experts disagree on whether the names should be revealed during the process or after it. The authors have found no significant advantage to either method. Each method has its list of advantages and disadvantages. The second-round results are again tallied. In Figure 5-9, the results show a difference from the first survey, indicating that the respondents changed their minds on the responses or were influenced by knowing the results from the first survey.

Step 7: Third-Round Survey and Tally

Once again a revised questionnaire is sent to the panel along with the results of the second round. The purpose of sending out three rounds of surveys is to have the panel of experts review the results of other experts and come to a consensus. There is usually some movement in the voting as the process continues.

While three or four rounds are normal, up to six have been conducted. This depends on the spread of the results and the enthusiasm of the panel of experts.

Step 8: Interpret the Results

As with any planning tool, the interpretation of the results is very important. The responses to the series of repeated survey questions enable a consensus process to take place. The result is a set of ideas, opinions, visions, or innovations that represent the best thinking of a group of experts that would not ordinarily come together to discuss the issue. The team will then take this series of questions, discuss their implications and use them in the next step of the planning process. The next tool can be Scenario Planning or Cross-Impact Analysis.

What Are Variations of this Tool?

The Delphi Technique is one of several techniques based upon group dynamics methods and designed to come to a consensus about a series of statements or questions. Another technique is the Nominal Group Technique (Millett and Honton 1991). The Nominal Group Technique is described in numerous books on forecasting or group dynamics.

References

"Analysis of Delphi Technique Survey." 1991. Cherry Hill Public Schools.

Armstrong, J. S. 1985. *Long-Range Forecasting: From Crystal Ball to Computer*, 2d ed. New York: John Wiley, Exhibit 14-1.

Dakley, N., and O. Helmer. 1963. "An Experimental Approach of the Delphi Method to the Use of Experts." *Management Science*, vol. 9, no. 3: 458.

Fildes, R. 1987. "Forecasting: The Issues." *The Handbook of Forecasting: A Manager's Guide*. New York: John Wiley & Sons., p. 161.

Kurtzman, J. 1984. *Futurcasting*. Palm Springs, CA: ETC Publications.

Makridakis, S., and S. C. Wheelwright. 1979. "Forecasting: Framework and Overview." *Forecasting*. Ed. S. Makridakis and S. C. Wheelwright. TIMS Studies in the Management Series, vol. 12, North-Holland, Amsterdam.

Millett, S. M., and E. J. Honton. 1991. *A Manager's Guide to Technology Forecasting and Statistical Analysis Methods*. Columbus: Battelle Press.

Ubben, G. 1997. *The Principalship: Creative Leadership for Effective Schools*. 3d ed. Needham Heights, MA: Allyn & Bacon.

Uchida, D., M. Cetron, and F. McKenzie. 1996. *Preparing Students for the 21st Century*. Arlington, VA: American Association of School Administrators.

Chapter 6

Morphological Analysis

A noted Swiss astrophysicist, Fritz Zwicky, developed a process to study the structural interrelationships of objects and phenomena during his early laboratory research in the 1940s. He called this Morphological Analysis. His first application of Morphological Analysis was on innovations in jet engines and rockets as a result of World War II. He later advocated the use of this process for problem solving in the sciences, mathematics, and in relationships in communities and social institutions. Morphology, the study of the basic patterns of things, was developed as a process for analyzing the structure and patterns of problems and creating multiple solutions that reflect an understanding and broad perspective of the problem area by the morphologist. The process works well in the fields of material objects, interrelationships, and phenomena. Morphologists feel that this analysis can be applied to any problem or subject, and it is generally recognized that this process can generate more potential solutions to problems than any other futuring tool. A key requirement of morphologists is an unbiased interest in the problem. It is essential that all bias, dogma, prejudice, and limitation of thought be set aside when conducting Morphological Analysis. A priori knowledge produces barriers when controls or restrictions are placed on the creation of alternative solutions.

What Is Its Purpose?

Morphological analysis is a systematic means of analyzing objects or products, processes, concepts, interrelationships, and phenomena. Its purpose is to discover the totality of all possible solutions to a problem through a careful analysis of the structure and patterns of the problem and the creative alternatives that are presented. Although this may not be possible in all cases, it is the goal of the morphologist.

Its specific purpose in this chapter is to present a systematic approach to futuring that provides the forecaster with a wide range of information concerning alternative futures. In this approach, the forecaster is required to consider all the possible options or solutions to a problem. This requirement reduces the tendency to eliminate potential solutions based upon prejudgment.

What Is Its Definition?

Zwicky defines morphology as "the development and practical application of basic methods which will allow us to discover and analyze the structure or morphological interrelationships among projects, phenomena, and concepts, and to explore the results gained for the construction of a sound world" (Zwicky 1969). The orientation of the morphologist must enable him or her to "visualize and comprehend all of the essential interrelations among physical objects, phenomena, concepts and ideas, as well as evaluate the human capabilities needed for all future constructive activities" (Zwicky 1969). For purposes of this book, Morphological Analysis is defined as the process of discovering and analyzing the form and structure of objects, interrelationships, and phenomena and to develop solutions to problems, issues, and inquiries in these areas.

What Are Its Operational Characteristics?

Morphological Analysis is a unique tool with characteristics and potential unlike many other futuring tools. The essential aspects of this approach are detailed in the following list.

1. Morphological research is a totality process. It intends to derive all the possible solutions to any given problem or issue and ensures that all aspects of any problem or issue will be thoroughly investigated.

2. The approach uses a Morphological Box or Matrix for the analysis. The Morphological Box is used to organize the structural parameters and elements of objects, interrelationships, and phenomena for analysis purposes. A matrix may be used where the structural parameters and elements are fewer in number.

3. Solutions derived from this analysis will be technologically and artistically complete. Because of the thoroughness of the analysis and the totality of the research, the solutions will be derived carefully, logically, and be acceptable to the user.

4. The morphological analysis provides more solutions than any other futuring tool. The versatility of this tool permits a very large number of ideas/solutions to be generated from the Morphological Box. The ideas/solutions may be identified selectively or at random.

5. The morphological approach provides a systematic process for invention and innovation. Rather than relying on haphazard trial and error techniques, this approach uses a rigorous and systematic process for creating new ideas and objects.

6. The process requires the user to be free to create. Morphologists must be free of dogma, bias, tradition, and any calcified beliefs that will inhibit their creative potential.

What Is Its Structure?

Morphological Analysis is accomplished by constructing a Morphological Box as shown in Figure 6-1. Objects, interrelationships, or phenomena are analyzed for their structural parameters, which are further analyzed for the elements that make up the parameters. The Morphological Box is constructed of several drawers stacked vertically, each representing a specific parameter and set of elements. The parameters are listed vertically and

$$P_{1.0} : E_{1.1}, \quad E_{1.2}, \quad E_{1.3}, \quad E_{1.4}, \quad E_{1.5}$$

$$P_{2.0} : E_{2.1}, \quad E_{2.2}, \quad E_{2.3}, \quad E_{2.4} \quad E_{2.5}$$

$$P_{3.0} : E_{3.1}, \quad E_{3.2}, \quad E_{3.3}$$

$$P_{4.0} : E_{4.1}, \quad E_{4.2}, \quad E_{4.3}, \quad E_{4.4}$$

$$P_{5.0} : E_{5.1}, \quad E_{5.2}, \quad E_{5.3}, \quad E_{5.4}$$

$$P_{6.0} : E_{6.1}, \quad E_{6.2}, \quad E_{6.3}$$

$$P_{7.0} : E_{7.1}, \quad E_{7.2}, \quad E_{7.3}$$

$$P_{8.0} : E_{8.1}, \quad E_{8.2}, \quad E_{8.3}, \quad E_{8.4}, \quad E_{8.5}$$

$$P_{9.0} : E_{9.1}, \quad E_{9.2}, \quad E_{9.3}, \quad E_{9.4}$$

$$P_{10.0} : E_{10.1}, \quad E_{10.2}, \quad E_{10.3}$$

Figure 6-1. The Morphological Box.

coded as P(1.0), P(2.0), P(3.0) and so on to distinguish them from each other. Within each drawer (or parameter) are elements including alternative elements that may reconfigure the parameter. The elements are noted by the taxonomic extensions such as 1.1, 1.2, 1.3, . . . 2.1, 2.2, 2.3, and the like. The taxonomic numbering system is preferred because of its unlimited numbering capability. Each is coded and distributed in the box, from which creative solutions are drawn by realigning the elements and parameters.

What Are Examples of Its Use?

Morphological Analysis involves finding widespread application to situations where a wide range of creative solutions are needed. Among these are engineering inventions; research in biology, physics, and chemistry; mathematics; linguistics; and the social sciences. This is especially true for the social scientists or social engineers who are constantly looking for innovative ways to solve our social dilemmas.

One example of the application of Morphological Analysis would be to examine the alternative interfaces between a college of education and public school systems in an attempt to establish a professional development

Parameters	Elements and Alternatives			
P(1.0) Number of School Systems	E(1.1) Single	E(1.2) Multiple		
P(2.0) Unit of a Public School	E(2.1) Role	E(2.2) Work group	E(2.3) Organizational Unit	E(2.4) Total Organization
P(3.0) Unit of a College	E(3.1) Role	E(3.2) Interest Group	E(3.3) Department Task Force	E(3.4) College Task Force
P(4.0) Need or purpose	E(4.1) Instruction	E(4.2) Service	E(4.3) Research	
P(5.0) Location or setting	E(5.1) College	E(5.2) Neutral Turf	E(5.3) Public School	

Figure 6-2. The Morphological Box: Parameters, elements, and alternatives. Courtesy of McCutchan Publishing Corp., 2526 Grove Street, Berkeley, CA 94704.

network. Among the major innovations in education recently is the forming of professional development networks between colleges of education and cooperating school districts in the surrounding geographic service area. There is a growing need for colleges to stay in continuous contact with public schools and share their needs and expertise in a partnership environment. This reciprocal relationship strengthens the effectiveness of the educational process.

Given the recognition of this need, the morphological approach raises the following questions: What are all the purposeful interfaces between public school systems and a college of education for professional development? Are there alternative interfaces to those that are being used presently? An analysis of this problem may be provided through the Morphological Box. Figure 6-2 shows the results of a morphological approach for developing purposeful interfaces between a college of education and public school systems. Possible solutions are determined by selecting one element (or alternative) from each parameter during a *pass*. Each pass will have a different combination of elements. Based upon the mathematical permutations of the elements, there are 288 possible solutions that may be extrapolated from the box.

Sometimes it is easier to work with the parameters and elements if they are rearranged in a multidimensional matrix. In this orientation, the parameters are listed horizontally across the top of the matrix. The elements are then listed vertically under each parameter for ease in connecting them. Figure 6-3 shows an example of the rearrangement of information from the Morphological Box (Figure 6-2) to the Morphological Matrix.

When the listing of all elements is complete, you can create new designs by selecting, either arbitrarily or systematically, one element from each parameter moving from left to right in the matrix. As noted earlier, this is called a pass, or more technically, an *extrapolation*. The first pass will produce a potential solution to the original question of how to increase and enhance the interface potential between a school district and a college of education.

One possible solution from this analysis is a consortium of *multiple* public school districts meeting as an *organizational unit* with college representatives to explore their respective *roles* for the purpose of providing professional *instruction* in a *neutral environment*. The meetings would be held at a neutral site (Hencley and Yates 1974).

Parameters (Design characteristics and requirements)

		Number of Public School Systems	Unit of a Public School	Unit of a College	Need or Purpose	Location or Setting of Interaction
Elements and Design	Alternatives	Single	Role	Role	Instruction	College
		Multiple	Work Group	Interest Group	Service	Neutral Turf
			Organizational Unit	Departmental Task Force	Research	Public School
			Total Organization	College Task Force		

Figure 6-3. The Morphological Matrix. Courtesy of McCutchan Publishing Corp. Courtesy of McCutchan Publishing Corp., 2526 Grove Street, Berkeley, CA 94704.

Other examples of applications of Morphological Analysis to education are in curriculum development, professional training of educational administrators, the design of new buildings and facilities, instructional areas where relationships among ideas, concepts, and issues are explored, and in developing a vision of the school's future.

What Is Its Process?

The Morphological Analysis process is simple in structure but has a variety of applications that differ according to the nature of the problem being analyzed. This chapter describes three primary applications of Morphological Analysis: (1) the design and redesign of objects; (2) an analysis of interrelationships of natural and contrived phenomena such as process improvement; and (3) an examination of ideas, concepts, and general abstract phenomena such as the development of an organization's future. Although the content or substance of problems in these three areas will vary, the process may be described generically at the outset and specifically as each area is explained independently.

Morphological Analysis	
Step 1:	Select the Appropriate Team
Step 2:	Formulate a clear and concise statement of the problem
Step 3:	Identify All the Important Parameters for the Problem Solution
Step 4:	Develop the Morphological Box or Matrix
Step 5:	Evaluate All Elements including Alternative Elements to Ascertain their Potential Performance and Ethical Value as a Solution
Step 6:	Select Multiple Solutions to the Problem
Step 7:	Prioritize Solutions based upon problem needs and field test Those with Highest Potential

Figure 6-4. Steps in developing a Morphological Analysis.

The Generic Process

There are seven primary steps in the overall process of Morphological Analysis. They are shown in Figure 6-4.

Each of these steps will be discussed in detail in the next three sections of the chapter.

Section 1: Morphological Analysis of Objects

This section explains how the Morphological Analysis process is used to create inventions, innovations, and new products or objects; to redesign existing objects; or to solve problems related to any one of these.

Step 1: Select the Appropriate Team

The focus of this process is to create or recreate tangible things such as those listed above. The team should include engineers from appropriate fields, such as civil, mechanical, industrial, chemical, electronic, or ergonomic, who have engineering expertise and experience with innovation and redesign. Other members of the team should include an experienced project manager, workers from the production, packaging, marketing, sales, and maintenance of the object, and representatives from those target functions that are affected by the object either in the plant or institution, or in the marketplace.

Step 2: Formulate a Clear and Concise Statement of the Problem

It is often said that a problem, clearly stated, is well on its way to a solution. In this case, a problem will be selected, concisely formulated, and analyzed to show the reader how the process works. For simplicity in understanding the process, the authors have chosen *writing instruments* as their object for analysis. Objects conforming to this concept are pencils, ballpoint and fountain pens, and felt-tip pens. There are mechanical as well as simple wooden pencils produced in a variety of shapes and quality for office work, school work, and carpentry, as well as novel designs for general marking. The analysis should address the development of a large number of new designs for a writing instrument. The primary need is as follows: The writing instrument must be lightweight for portability, attractive, and easily manipulated and stored. It must contain few parts and mark on any surface. The problem will be stated as follows: *What are all the purposive alternative designs for a writing instrument?*

Step 3: Identify All the Important Parameters for the Problem Solution

The term *parameter* is important here because the selection of parameters is critical to the value of the solutions generated. A parameter is a primary descriptor within an object that assists in determining the specific form and pattern of the object but not its general nature. Metaphorically, parameters of the human body would include the systems of bones, muscles, blood and fluids, organs, respiratory, and waste. The body's general nature evolves when the elements of these parameters are assembled into new configurations, which are reflected in the appearance, movements, size, shape, and other characteristics of the body.

Parameters are referred to as "pegs of knowledge," or facts that form the critical structure of the object. For instance, lightweight is a "peg" for a writing instrument. In order to generate all the possible alternatives to a writing instrument, parameters may be added to or deleted from existing instruments to free the morphological process to create new solutions. Pegs, however, are those parameters that are essential to all alternative designs for this object. Additional parameters may be included to provide greater design options. The relationship of the pegs and additional parameters to the problem is illustrated in Figure 6-5. The parameters chosen for this problem are:

P(1.0) Weight in ounces

P(2.0) Shape

P(3.0) Color

P(4.0) Material

P(5.0) Marking substance

P(6.0) Number of parts

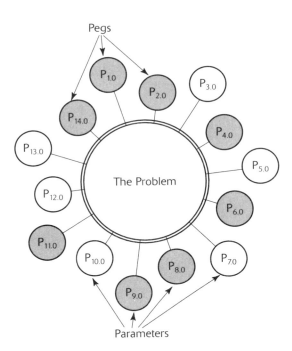

Figure 6-5. Relationship of the parameters to the problem. ("Pegs" are identified by the shading of parameters.)

P(7.0) Storage

P(8.0) Auxiliary functions

Step 4: Develop the Morphological Box or Matrix

Once the parameters are identified, the Morphological Box may be developed. The parameters are listed vertically and labeled P(1.0) and so on, as shown earlier. Each parameter is identified by a title that is written beside its number. See example in Figure 6-6. The parameter elements are placed in the box as shown.

An *element* is a component or constituent of the parameter and an entity that satisfies all the conditions of belonging to that parameter. Elements may be considered *design alternatives* when analyzing an object because of the physical and functional design changes involved. Certain or all elements in each parameter may be retained to preserve those design functions that are satisfactory to users. New elements in the form of design alternatives are added to give the object potentially new forms and functions. Added elements must fall within the guidelines set by the parameters and be clustered within the appropriate parameter. Figure 6-7 illustrates the clustering of elements within a parameter.

An example may be found in the common analog clock. Although there are many different designs for clocks, they all have similar parameters and elements. An analog clock, for instance, has several basic parameters: P(1.0), pointing devices that point to the time. P(2.0), a number or symbol representing time; P(3.0), a power source to make it run; and P(4.0), an encasement or framed structure to house it. Elements under P(2.0) might be simple numbers or Roman numerals. Alternative elements might include jeweled dots, letters of the alphabet, humorous symbols, pictures of animals, and the like. Mixing the regular elements with alternative elements provides more flexibility for creative solutions.

The design team has the option of using the Morphological Box or the Morphological Matrix shown in Figure 6-8. When using the matrix, the locations of the parameters and elements are very clear and the P and E coding system is unnecessary. The matrix can be constructed more quickly and seems to have greater "user-friendly" advantage.

Problem: What are all the possible purposive alternatives for a writing implement?

Parameters		Elements or Design Alternatives			
P(1.0)	Weight	E(1.1) 0.0 Ounces	E(1.2) 0.10 Oz.	E(1.3) 0.25 Oz.	E(1.4) 0.50 Oz.
P(2.0)	Shape	E(2.1) Round	E(2.2) Square	E(2.3) Oval	E(2.4) Rectangular
P(3.0)	Color	E(3.1) Red	E(3.2) Green	E(3.3) Yellow	E(3.4) Blue
P(4.0)	Material	E(4.1) Metal	E(4.2) Plastic	E(4.3) Ceramic	E(4.4) Porcelain
P(5.0)	Marking Substance	E(5.1) Graphite	E(5.2) Ink	E(5.3) Paint	E(5.4) Laser
P(6.0)	Number of Parts	E(6.1) One	E(6.2) Two	E(6.3) Three	E(6.4) Four
P(7.0)	Storage	E(7.1) In Box	E(7.2) In Pocket	E(7.3) On Belt	E(7.4) On Lapel
P(8.0)	Additional Functions	E(8.1) Key Chain	E(8.2) Pocket Knife	E(8.3) Paper-weight	E(8.4) Self-Standing

Parameters		Elements or Design Alternatives			
P(1.0)	Weight	E(1.5) 0.75 Oz.	E(1.6) 1 Ounce	E(1.7) 2 Ounces	E(1.8) 3 Ounces
P(2.0)	Shape	E(2.5) Octagonal	E(2.6) Hexagonal	E(2.7) Ribbed	E(2.8) Curled
P(3.0)	Color	E(3.5) Violet	E(3.6) Gold	E(3.7) Silver	E(3.8) Gray
P(4.0)	Material	E(4.5) Wood	E(4.6) Leather	E(4.7) Glass	E(4.8) Fiberglass
P(5.0)	Marking Substance	E(5.5) Chalk	E(5.6) Dye	E(5.7) Etcher	E(5.8) Powder
P(6.0)	Number of Parts	E(6.5) Five	E(6.6) Six	E(6.7) Seven	
P(7.0)	Storage	E(7.5) Around Neck	E(7.6) Attached to Arm	E(7.7) In Shoe	E(7.8) Inside Clothes
P(8.0)	Additional Functions	E(8.5) Calculator	E(8.6) Digital Clock E(8.7)		

Figure 6-6. Morphological Box for writing instrument.

Parameters		Elements or Design Alternatives						
P(1.0)	Weight	E(1.9)	4 Ounces					
P(2.0)	Shape	E(2.9)	Free-form					
P(3.0)	Color	E(3.9)	Brown	E(3.10)	Orange	E(3.11)	Turquoise	E(3.12)	Black
P(4.0)	Material	E(4.9)	Styrofoam	E(4.10)	Rubber	E(4.11)	Cardboard	
P(5.0)	Marking Substance							
P(6.0)	Number of Parts							
P(7.0)	Storage							
P(8.0)	Additional Functions							

Parameters		Elements or Design Alternatives	
P(1.0)	Weight		
P(2.0)	Shape		
P(3.0)	Color	E(3.13)	White
P(4.0)	Material		
P(5.0)	Marking Substance		
P(6.0)	Number of Parts		
P(7.0)	Storage		
P(8.0)	Additional Functions		

Figure 6-6. Morphological Box for writing instrument *(continued)*.

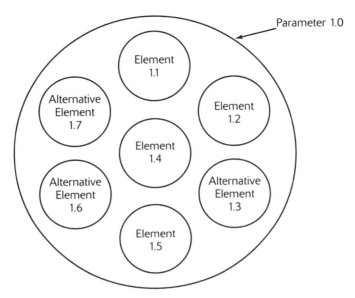

Figure 6-7. Elements and alternative elements are parts of parameters.

The parameters and their elements are rearranged into the matrix format in Figure 6-8 and are now ready to be evaluated in terms of their potential performance and ethical value as a solution.

Step 5: Evaluate all Elements including Alternative Elements to Ascertain their Potential Performance and Ethical Value as a Solution

Not every solution to a problem is good. This applies to Morphological Analysis as well as other problem-solving procedures. The potential performance and ethical value of solutions to be generated by the box or matrix needs to be considered at this time. Assuming the matrix contains all the possible parameters and elements necessary for creating myriad new designs for a writing instrument, what then will be the guidelines for creating and selecting these new designs for performance and ethical value?

This question is answered by the identification of a set of values established by the team to be used as guidelines in assessing the appropriateness of the parameters and elements in the matrix and the new designs produced.

Problem: What are all the possible purposive alternatives for a writing instrument?

Parameters	Weight	Shape	Color	Material	Marking substance	Number of parts	Storage	Auxiliary Function
	0 ounces	round	red	metal	graphite	1	in box	key chain
	.10 ounces	square	green	plastic	ink	2	in pocket	pocket knife
	.25 ounces	oval	yellow	ceramic	paint	3	on belt	paperweight
	.50 ounces	rectangular	blue	porcelain	laser	4	on lapel	self-standing
	.75 ounces	octagonal	violet	wood	chalk	5	around neck	calculator
	1 ounce	hexagonal	gold	leather	dye	6	attach to arm	digital clock
	2 ounces	ribbed	silver	glass	etcher	7	in shoe	
	3 ounces	curled	gray	fiberglass	powder		inside clothes	
	4 ounces	free-form	brown	styrofoam				
		flat	orange	rubber				
			turquoise	cardboard				
			black					
			white					

Design Elements and Alternatives

The new design is a _____ ounce, _____, _____, _____ marker with _____ parts that can be stored _____ and an auxiliary function as _____.

Figure 6-8. Morphological Matrix analysis for writing instrument.

The morphological process has a tendency to produce a large variety of potential solutions, some of which may be untimely or too costly, require resources not yet available, or be basically unacceptable to the user. It is at this point in the process that each element or design alternative is assessed for acceptable inclusion. The generic focus is to determine whether the element will contribute positively and efficiently to a solution, and to what extent the solution will be ethically sound.

For example, consider the matrix in Figure 6-8. The Weight parameter lists weights from 0.0 to 4.0 ounces. A performance assessment may very well rule out 0.0, 0.10, and 0.25 ounces as viable elements. In the Shape parameter, the team may remove from consideration "free form" and "curled" as undesirable. "Styrofoam" may be dropped from Materials as well as "powder" from Marking Substance. These omissions reduce the number of superfluous designs that would not satisfy the performance and ethical value tests. The generic focus, again, is to determine whether the element will contribute positively and efficiently to a solution, and to what extent the solution will be ethically sound.

The design team needs to identify a set of assessment criteria to determine the value of each element as part of a design solution. These criteria may be brainstormed through various means and prioritized for more accurate evaluation. A sample list of criteria follows:

The writing instrument indicated by the solutions should be:

- portable

- appealing to the user

- easily held and manipulated by the fingers

- able to write on any or most surfaces

- easily stored on a person

- reasonably priced

- durable

- marketable

- competitive

This realm of values may be determined by using the Nominal Group Technique or some form of multi-voting to produce a firm set of values for assessment. The assessment may be done in a decision-making matrix where each parameter and element can be scrutinized against each value. Elements not meeting all or portions of these criteria should be reconsidered and possibly withdrawn from the matrix. Replacement elements may be available; otherwise, the parameter will have one less element for consideration.

Step 6: Select Multiple Solutions to the Problem

This is an interesting and fun step. Figure 6.8 presents a completed matrix for a writing instrument. The matrix has eight parameters each with a list of six or more elements. The total number of potential solutions that can be obtained from this matrix is calculated by multiplying the number of elements in each parameter as follows:

P(1.0)	P(2.0)	P(3.0)	P(4.0)	P(5.0)	P(6.0)	P(7.0)	P(8.0)

$$9 \times 10 \times 13 \times 11 \times 8 \times 7 \times 8 \times 6 = 34{,}594{,}560 \text{ solutions}$$

One can easily see that this is an enormous number of solutions. This number suggests that elements must be carefully selected on each pass, based upon their potential performance and ethical value.

Solutions are determined by selecting one element from each of the eight parameters that collectively form a new solution. This constitutes one extrapolation or pass in the matrix. More than one element may be selected from any parameter during any pass. One reason for this is that, for instance, the solution may require two (or more) colors to enhance its market value. Additional materials may also be required for added strength and endurance. There are no restrictions on this. The second and ensuing extrapolations are done using the same procedure until all possible solutions have been pulled from the matrix. Elements may be selected either randomly or purposively from their parameters and connections are forced. Each extrapolation must have at least one different element to create a different solution. The permutations of the elements become obvious as each pass is made. Each new design solution is stated in the format shown at the bottom of the matrix in Figure 6-8. For example, the first pass might produce a: *1-ounce, flat, black, plastic, ink marker* with *three parts* that can be stored *in a pocket*, and has an auxiliary function as a *key chain*.

Ensuing passes will produce thousands of new designs from this single Matrix. This process is sometimes referred to as *forced connections*, since the elements are selected from each column and essentially forced together to form a new whole.

Step 7: Prioritize Solutions Based upon Problem Needs and Field-Test those with Highest Potential

After the desired number of passes or extrapolations are made from the matrix, the new designs are listed for prioritization by the team. This may be done using the Prioritization Matrix, a Nominal Group Technique, or a simple multi-vote procedure. See the *Memory Jogger II* booklet by GOAL/QPC for descriptions of these tools. The team may then select the top few potential solutions and develop prototypes for field testing. The final solution(s) will be determined from the field test results.

Section 2: Morphological Analysis of Interrelationships among Phenomena

A second way to apply the Morphological Analysis is to examine relationships among such fields as physical and social phenomena; natural and contrived phenomena such as scientific and technological interfaces; economic phenomena relating to production, transportation, and services; and communications. The objective of this second field of focus is the same as the first, namely, the development of all the purposive solutions that show promise of improving the interrelationships between and among these phenomena. The process is fundamentally the same, except for the content of the Morphological Box or Matrix.

This section will focus on the interrelationships of a series of events and activities that interface economics, communications, and social phenomena.

Among the key processes in most organizations is the employment process. This process is selected for illustration here because it is generic to industrial, governmental, health care, and educational organizations, and represents a competitive need to seek and employ the type of individuals who will maintain quality service to customers during the next decade and beyond. The following steps are repeated from Section 1 to explain how the analysis works in the context of interrelationships of phenomena.

Step 1: Select the Appropriate Team

Members of the team should represent the offices of human resources or personnel, administration and finance, senior executive administrators, work supervisors, and selected colleagues with whom the newly hired will work. Other members may be added as desired.

Step 2: Formulate a Clear and Concise Statement of the Problem

The generic employment process for most organizations consists of three fundamental segments: (1) the receipt and review of applications; (2) the interview procedure; and (3) the employment orientation and documentation. A flowchart of these three segments is presented in Figure 6-9. It is important to note here that the flowchart has a formal structure with different symbols reflecting activities and events. The straight horizontal line, for example, is a symbol for activity. The rectangle depicts an event that either has happened or will happen. The diamond shape means that a decision is made, usually for approval or disapproval. Oval shapes usually indicate the beginning and ending of the flowchart. The three segments in this chart reflect a total process. Each segment is considered a subprocess. The most critical and time-consuming part of the employment process is the interview procedure; therefore, the analysis will be done on that segment.

The problem may be stated as follows: *What are all the possible purposive alternatives for making the future employment process more effective and efficient?*

Step 3: Identify All the Important Parameters for the Problem Solution

Selection of the parameters requires careful consideration and identification of the "pegs" explained earlier in the chapter. The pegs are critical pieces of the overall process and are broadly interrelated with the application and

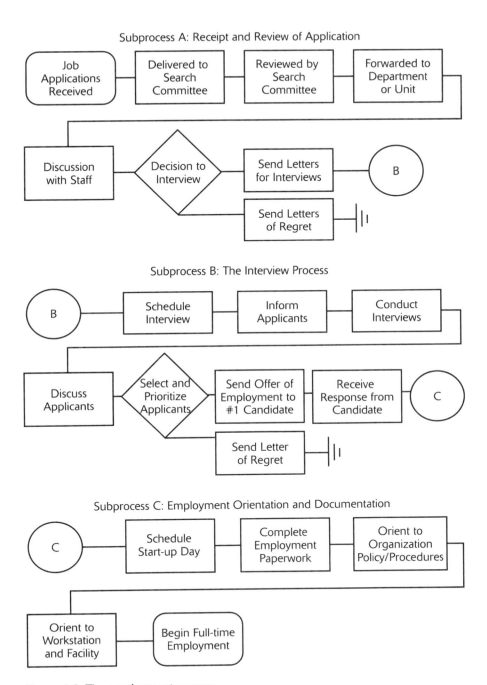

Figure 6-9. The employment process.

employment orientation segments. Ideas for other parameters may be obtained by benchmarking other similar organizations. Eight parameters are identified in the flowchart for the interview segment. Several of these are considered pegs and are essential to the segment. Others are included in the flowchart because they have greater flexibility for variation and improvement. The following parameters are recommended (See Figure 6-9):

P(1.0) Arrange scheduled interviews

P(2.0) Inform applicants

P(3.0) Conduct interviews

P(4.0) Discuss applicants

P(5.0) Select/prioritize candidates

P(6.0) Notify candidate #1 with offer of employment

P(7.0) Notify remaining candidates with regrets

P(8.0) Receive response from candidate #1.

Step 4: Develop the Morphological Box or Matrix

Now that the parameters have been identified for the interview segment, the elements may be added. The Morphological Matrix is used because the arrangement of the information in horizontal flowchart format is beneficial. The graphic structure of the matrix is varied to accommodate the flowchart. The continued development of new technology allows more freedom to create in some areas; therefore, elements are listed vertically under those parameters targeted for improvement. Since the problem is to develop "all the possible alternative solutions," the elements will include negative as well as positive items. See Figure 6-10. It is the responsibility of the team to develop the assessment values to screen out those elements that contribute little or nothing to improving the process.

Schedule Interviews	Inform Applicants	Conduct Interviews	Discuss Applicants	Select/Prioritize Applicants	Send Offer of Employment (Candidate)	Send Regrets to others	Receive Response from Candidate
P(1.0)	P(2.0)	P(3.0)	P(4.0)	P(5.0)	P(6.0)	P(7.0)	P(8.0)
1.1 With search committee	2.1 By E-mail	3.1 By conference call	4.1 In group meeting	5.1 Use Nominal Group Technique	6.1 By telephone	7.1 By telephone	8.1 By telephone
1.2 With all employees in large meeting	2.2 By telephone	3.2 By E-mail	4.2 By conference call	5.2 Use multivote	6.2 By certified mail	7.2 By certified mail	8.2 By certified mail
	2.3 By fax	3.3 Home interview by computer	4.3 By E-mail	5.3 Use prioritization matrix	6.3 By E-mail	7.3 By 1st class mail	8.3 By fax
1.3 Simultaneous interview with spouse	2.4 By overnite express	3.4 Full day on site with all employees	4.4 Hold open meetings with employees	5.4 Vote by units	6.4 By courier	7.4 With flowers or fruit basket	8.4 In person
	2.5 By courier	3.5 Off site in restaurant or hotel room	4.5 By individual summary letters or forms	5.5 Establish criteria with employees	6.5 By telegram	7.5 Personalized letter from CEO	8.5 By courier
1.4 One-on-one meetings with key administrator	2.6 By telegram	3.6 Contract service with professional group	4.6 Contact references for discussion		6.6 By 1st class mail	7.6 Have secretary send form letter	8.6 By letter from candidate and spouse
	2.7 Provide applicant with info packet	3.7 Use videotaped procedure			6.7 Send info on benefits		
1.5 Schedule series of short meetings throughout day for open interviews	2.8 Employer visit to home office of applicant	3.8 On site with key administrators			6.8 Request second interview for top candidate		
	2.9 Request portfolios of experience	3.9 During meeting of Board					
1.6 Schedule two days of interviews for each applicant		3.10 Conduct series of "coffee klatch" meetings for employees					

Figure 6-10. A Morphological Matrix for subprocess B: The interview process.

Step 5: Evaluate All Elements including Alternative Elements to Ascertain their Potential Performance and Ethical Value as a Solution

A set of criteria must be developed by the team to assess the parameters and elements in the matrix prior to making the extrapolations or passes. Criteria that are specific to this analysis might be:

- Time consumed

- Cost

- Number of people required

- Accuracy of the interviewers

- Convenience of interview sites or locations

- Avoidance of duplication

- Efficiency of communications procedures

- Linkages with segments 1 and 3

- Consistency with organizational practice

- Ability to enhance the process

Step 6: Select Multiple Solutions to the Problem

It is recommended that each pass be conducted carefully by the team, in order to give consideration to all the possible interrelationships that can be affected by the results of the pass. Some elements may be strongly linked with others and work together harmoniously. Avoid those elements that do not work well together. It is this holistic character that becomes important in the analysis. Ideally, each pass should be roughly flowcharted to monitor any resulting bottlenecks, waste points, duplications, or other negative influences. The passes made on this matrix have considerably more to be concerned with than those made when redesigning an object, as in Section 1.

Step 7: Prioritize Solutions Based upon Problem Needs and Field Test Those with Highest Potential

After the most desirable extrapolations are made from the matrix, the team must review them critically for prioritization and implementation. A Nominal Group Technique or multi-vote by team members will identify the top three alternative flowcharts. From there, the organizational membership may be informed and asked to voice their opinion on the top choices.

Section 3: Morphological Analysis of Interrelationships among Abstractions

It is this third application of Morphological Analysis that examines how to use the tool to develop a vision or forecast of the future of an organization. The interrelationships of abstractions is the most complex and intricate field to analyze and requires a process that incorporates totality research. As Zwicky says, "In my opinion it is the morphologists' unbiased and comprehensive way of seeing things that promises to contribute the most to the integral treatment of complex problems" (1969). The advantage of the morphologist is that he or she can analyze any field, problem, or phenomenon, whether fully knowledgeable of that field or not, by researching those universal structural characteristics which compose the field of study. This is important to Section 3, where the task is to start from scratch and generate a vision for an organization. The following steps are used to accomplish this task.

Step 1: Select the Appropriate Team

The team assigned the task of developing its organization's vision will likely be more generic in its membership than in the two prior applications of Morphological Analysis. In this case, there is a strong need for cross-functional representation, particularly from such areas as leadership/management, human resources, line employees, staff, customers, and stakeholders. Many organizations discover that they have intuitive thinkers among their employ who may contribute greatly to the futuring task.

Step 2: Formulate a Clear and Concise Statement of the Problem

The problem may be clearly stated as *What are all the purposive alternative futures for this organization?* The problem is stated broadly to include consideration of all solutions that might be generated, analyzed, and evaluated. Searching for all solutions minimizes the chances of overlooking a promising alternative future.

Step 3: Identify All the Important Parameters for the Problem Solution

The team should begin to investigate the universal structural characteristics of visions, forecasts, and statements of the future from other organizations that are both similar and dissimilar. Add to this any peculiar structural components of vision statements for your organization, if available. This procedure will provide the team with those universal parameters essential to identifying all the possible alternative futures.

Examples of parameters that may be used for developing alternative futures are:

$P(1.0)$: The designated point of time in the future when the vision will materialize.

$P(2.0)$: Specific events likely to be in place that will characterize the *external environment* of the organization at that future time point. This will consider such areas as demographics, resources, values/lifestyles, technology, public attitudes, political actions, economics, the workforce, and global impact.

$P(3.0)$: Specific conditions likely to be in place that will characterize the *internal environment* of the organization at that future time point. Consider such things as the organization's culture, personnel, administration/leadership, employees, facilities, curriculum, instructional programs, budgets/funding, technology applications, and community relations.

$P(4.0)$: Those major influential forces that will cause the organization to move toward an alternative future. These forces may be in place presently or develop as the organization moves toward the future time point. Examples include regulations from local, state, and national governments; technological innovations; demographic changes in the community; resource allocations and reserves; community and state funding; and visionary leadership.

Step 4: Develop the Morphological Box or Matrix

Although the parameters and elements may be displayed in the Morphological Box, it will be easier to work with this information in the Morphological Matrix format. The analysis of abstractions, that is, alternative futures, will cause a larger number of elements than normal to be listed under each parameter. This is due to the complexity of the problem and the nature of the Morphological Analysis tool. The matrix, therefore, will contain fewer parameters and considerably more elements from which to choose. There will also be a larger number of elements selected from the parameters during each extrapolation, in order to piece together the complex alternative futures sought from the matrix. Figure 6-11 shows an example of a partial matrix for developing alternative futures.

Step 5: Evaluate all Elements including Alternative Elements to Ascertain their Potential Performance and Ethical Value as a Solution

The team has the responsibility for composing a list of criteria that can be used to assess the elements in the matrix. The extent of the list will vary from organization to organization with emphases given to different elements based upon the size and location of the organization. For instance, assessing an urban school district or college will vary somewhat from assessing suburban institutions, depending upon the community each serves and the resources available. Possible criteria might be:

- Is the element future-oriented?

- Can the element be achieved within the future time period?

- Is there duplication or overlap in the elements?

P(1.0) Designated Future Time	P(2.0) Major Causal Forces	P(3.0) Specific Events in the External Environment	P(4.0) Specific Events in the Internal Environment
1.1 Three years	2.1 Decrease in state funding for education.	3.1 Alternate sources of funding through partnerships.	4.1 District decentralizes through site-based management.
1.2 Five years	2.2 Decrease in gubernatorial support for education.	3.2 State-mandated core curriculum.	4.2 Use of Baldrige quality achievement.
1.3 Ten years	2.3 Changes in state certification standards.	3.3 Establishment of local charter schools.	4.3 Increased enrollments in school-to-work programs.
1.4 Fifteen years	2.4 Mandated emphasis on equity and diversity.	3.4 Increase in private and parochial schools.	4.4 Increased involvement in Professional Development Networks.
	2.5 Increased legislative regulation of districts.	3.5 School districts operated by contract with private groups.	4.5 Increase in overall school enrollments.
	2.6 Significant increase in Hispanic population.	3.6 Spanish required as second language in U.S.	4.6 Child care programs established in districts.
	2.7 Increasing numbers of citizens in "senior" age groups.	3.7 School voucher systems established.	4.7 Increased afterschool programs and activities scheduled for the community.
	2.8 More than 50% of workers between 1990–2005 will be minorities.	3.8 Access to World Wide Web available to all students, faculty, and staff.	4.8 Virtual reality techniques used in sciences.
	2.9 Growing national support for year-round schools.	3.9 Development of the computerized home learning center.	(Etcetera)
	2.10 Increasing advances in technology.	3.10 Increase in alternative schooling.	
	2.11 Increased influence for change by consultants, scholars, and leaders.	3.11 Expanded national testing.	
	(Etcetera)	(Etcetera)	

Figure 6-11. Partial matrix of alternative futures.

- Are elements reasonably predictable or are they uncertain?

- Can the available and anticipated resources support the elements?

Step 6: Select Multiple Solutions to the Problem

The matrix generated in this problem will produce an extremely large number of alternative futures requiring analysis and evaluation. This is a formidable task for any team. In this field of morphological research, a variation in the process is recommended in order to identify a few highly probable futures that are realistic to the organization. This variation is called *modest morphology*. This concept was offered by Professor John Strong of Johns Hopkins University while serving as Vice-President of the International Society for Morphological Research (Zwicky 1969, p. 259).

Modest morphology suggests that prior to the extrapolations, the team should study the parameters and elements carefully to ascertain anticipated advantages and disadvantages, possibility or impossibility, acceptability or nonacceptability, and so on, of the choices. The team may proceed to extrapolate one or more *preferred futures* from the alternatives in the matrix.

This may be followed by extrapolating a group of roughly three to six *probable futures* for consideration. As a back-up strategy, it is recommended that two to three *possible futures* be determined, in the event that none of those in the preferred or probable categories are achievable.

This procedure should provide approximately ten alternative futures for the organization. The value in identifying these priority levels of the organization's future is that better control may be administered as the organization moves toward a clearly defined and fully supported vision of its future.

Step 7: Prioritize Solutions Based upon Problem Needs and Field-Test those with Highest Potential

The alternative futures are extrapolated from the matrix in order of desirability. The descriptions in Step 6 instruct the team to select one or more preferred futures, followed by three to six probable futures, followed by two to three possible futures.

The field-testing component involves certain steps that the team is obligated to pursue. They are:

- Obtain approval and support for the selected vision.

- Identify strategic initiatives and strategies for achieving the preferred vision.

- Develop the organization's long-range plan, including goals, objectives, and activities that lead the organization toward the vision.

- Deploy the long-range plan throughout the organization.

- Develop a tactical or business plan to prepare the organization for movement toward the vision.

- Develop and monitor annual plans for achievement of long-range goals and objectives.

What Are Variations of this Tool?

An interesting variation in the morphological process is the Multidimensional matrix analysis. This process allows the analyst(s) to simultaneously examine the interrelationships among three or more elements extrapolated from their parameters. For example, the Multidimensional matrix in Figure 6-12 has three dimensions utilizing three parameters. The parameters are distinguished as before, namely, P(1.0), P(2.0), and P(3.0).

Several elements have been identified for each parameter and shown in the matrix as E1.1, E(1.2), E(1.3), E(1.4), E(1.5), and E(1.6) on the y axis; followed by E(2.1), E(2.2), E(2.3), E(2.4), E(2.5), and E(2.6) on the x axis; followed by E(3.1), E(3.2), E(3.3), E(3.4), and E(3.5) on the z axis. Metaphorically, this design creates a box structure with 36 drawers and 180 compartments containing the parameter components. The sample drawer that appears to be pulled out has five compartments with the following interfacing elements:

- Compartment one contains elements E(1.6), E(2.6), and E(3.1).

- Compartment two contains elements E(1.6), E(2.6), and E(3.2).

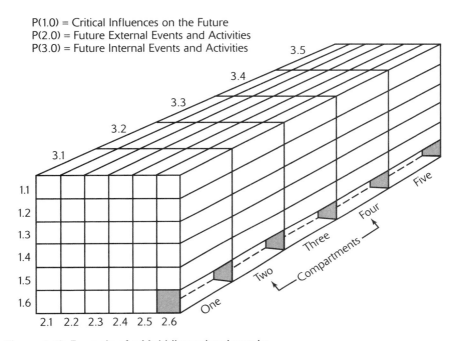

P(1.0) = Critical Influences on the Future
P(2.0) = Future External Events and Activities
P(3.0) = Future Internal Events and Activities

Figure 6-12. Example of a Multidimensional matrix.

- Compartment three contains elements E(1.6), E(2.6), and E(3.3).

- Compartment four contains elements E(1.6), E(2.6), and E(3.4).

- Compartment five contains elements E(1.6), E(2.6), and E(3.5).

This matrix design is suitable for analyzing abstract phenomena because of its ability to interface elements simultaneously. It would also be helpful for developing an organization's vision, since it provides a means of considering a large number of possible interrelationships among alternatives.

References

Brassard, M., and D. Ritter. 1994. *The Memory Jogger II*. Methuen, MA: GOAL/QPC.

Ignatovich, F. R. 1974. "Morphological Analysis," Chapter 10 in *Futurism in Education* by Henclay and Yates. Berkeley, CA: McCutcheon Publishing Corporation, p. 211–233.

Jones, H., and B. C. Twiss. 1978. *Forecasting Technology for Planning Decisions*. New York: Petrocelli Books.

Wheelwright, S. C., and S. Makridakis. 1985. *Forecasting Methods For Management*. New York: John Wiley & Sons, p. 10–19.

Zwicky, F. 1969. *Invention, Research, Through the Morphological Approach*. Toronto: MacMillan.

Zwicky, F. 1962. "Morphology of Propulsive Power," *Monographs on Morphological Research*. No. 1. Pasadena, CA: Society for Morphological Research.

Chapter 7

Crawford Slip Method

The Crawford Slip Method (CSM) provides an orderly procedure for collecting creative ideas from both individuals and groups and systematically processing these ideas to solve a problem or develop a desired result. This chapter describes how this method may be used to forecast a vision for an organization.

What Is Its Purpose?

The Crawford Slip Method is a technique for gathering and organizing a large number of ideas. Developed by Claude C. Crawford in 1925, the method collects ideas that have been brainstormed by individuals independently, simultaneously, anonymously, and rapidly in a "think tank" environment. Crawford's method systematically organizes a large number of ideas in a very short time and reorganizes these ideas into specific suggestions for performance improvement as well as identifying anchor points for vision development.

CSM is based on a theory known as Paired Association Paradigm, which employs a six-stage process of memory cue and retrieval similar to computer database function. Operationally, CSM stimulates retrieval of knowledge and expertise from human long-term memory using carefully constructed questions (Dettmer, Krone, and Gould 1989).

In practice, CSM supports the fundamental premise that people in an organization have untapped knowledge and expertise which, through meaningful participation in problem solving and management decision-making activities, creates a vested interest in ensuring that the organization has constancy of purpose.

What Is Its Definition?

The Crawford Slip Method is a process for systematically collecting creative ideas from individuals or groups, organizing these ideas, and proposing a plan to solve a problem or develop results for a predetermined goal. The process consists of identifying a general need, stating that need as one or more targets, writing ideas on slips, classifying the slips, and drafting a plan of action incorporating the ideas collected.

What Are Its Operational Characteristics?

The Crawford Slip Method has several distinct advantages in its design that make it a very useful tool for all levels of future planning.

1. Conserves time. CSM maximizes the effective use of time, one of the most valuable resources available. The process can focus the brainpower and energy of a group intensively on an issue in as little as ten to fifteen minutes. It is a simple process to follow and yields a large amount of information.

2. Focuses effort. The CSM process is a personalized, writing-based process, and therefore avoids the verbal discussions, debates, and confrontations that often occur when brainstorming is done verbally. Participants' efforts are independently focused on the primary issues in the process which tends to exclude unrelated issues. No constraints are placed on creativity.

3. Preserves anonymity. Since all slips are the same size, color, and format, and are not signed, individual identity is unknown. This enables participants to be free to suggest creative ideas without fear of criticism or reprisal. It has been found that participants will write

things on anonymous slips that they would not contribute in open discussion. This increases the quality of the ideas generated in the process.

4. Provides a solution and an action plan to implement the solution. Once the problem targets are identified and proposed solutions gathered from the slip writing, a detailed action plan is written to implement the solutions and assess their effectiveness in solving the targeted needs.

What Is Its Structure?

The Crawford Slip Method employs six fundamental steps, beginning with the identification of a recognized need or concern. This *need* is then diagnosed and restated as *targets*. Following the target planning, slip writing and classification are conducted to form the foundation of the planning team's report. An Action Instrument is then prepared followed by an assessment procedure (Dettmer, Krone, and Gould 1989). Figure 7-1 presents a model of the CSM.

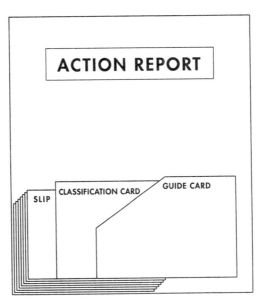

Figure 7-1. The Crawford Slip model.

What Are Examples of Its Use?

Uses of the Crawford Slip Method are numerous. It has had wide applications in a number of areas. Most common among them are the development of training materials and programs for fire department personnel, police, city government officials, civil defense personnel, nursing home administrators, vocational teachers, and veterans.

Among the recent applications was the development of state curriculum guides in Health Occupations and Cosmetology training in the public schools of New Jersey. The Health Occupations program was very complex and drew information from approximately 125 health occupations, resulting in twenty-two themes. These themes were further analyzed and sequenced by level of difficulty and assembled into a State Curriculum Guide. The Guide was implemented on a field-test basis, revised and published as the official Guide for the State.

The CSM has also been used in the development of new products in the chemical and diamond industries. The advantages of speed, intense focus on target problems, and the efficient development and implementation of action plans make this tool flexible and adaptable to many applications.

What Is Its Process?

The Crawford Slip Method is simple and action-oriented. It employs the brainstorming process but adds structure and refinement to the selected results. CSM works well with future planning teams. Its procedure is outlined in Figure 7-2.

Step 1: Assemble the Future Planning Team

The first step is to identify the organization's need or concern that is to be addressed. This need is then restated in one or more "How To" statements or questions. At this point, consideration for team membership should be given to those who have the knowledge and experience to deal with the futuring questions. In many cases the need will automatically suggest suitable candidates for participation in the process. In this example, the need is to develop an organization's vision projecting ten years into the future.

Crawford Slip Method	
Step 1:	Assemble the Future Planning Team
Step 2:	Identify Primary and Ancillary Targets
Step 3:	Conduct the Slip Writing
Step 4:	Sort the Slips and Determine Major Themes
Step 5:	Develop the Action Plan
Step 6:	Implement the Action Plan

Figure 7-2. Steps in developing the Crawford Slip Method.

Step 2: Identify Primary and Ancillary Targets

The need is initially expressed in a descriptive term or short phrase followed by one or more statements or questions directed at the need. These typically begin with "How To" and are called *targets*. An example of a need statement might be *Preparing for the next decade*. An example of a target might be *How to forecast a ten-year vision for the organization*. Ancillary target statements further diagnose the need. Examples might include *How to analyze future customer needs*, or *How to maintain continuous improvement in the organization's processes and infrastructure*. These and perhaps other targets approach the selected need from several directions, which, collectively, provide a reasonably accurate diagnosis. This expression of the need and target questions is referred to by CSM experts as brainpower networking.

Step 3: Conduct the Slip Writing

The next step is to conduct what is called the *slip writing*. It is important that participants understand this step to avoid confusion. Participants are given a brief orientation by the facilitator, who is responsible for the integrity of the entire method. Following the orientation, team members are given 20 to 30 slips of paper approximately 2¾″ by 4¼″ in size. These sizes are based on a standard 8½″ by 11″ sheet cut into equal pieces. If preferred, 3″ by 5″ cards may be used.

The first target is read by the facilitator and includes any ancillary targets. Team members are given approximately 10 minutes to write ideas that respond to the target question on the slips. For example, a target question related to vision might be *How to forecast a ten-year vision for the organization.* Examples of ideas on slips might read as follows: *analyze technological changes occurring in the organization; project possible employee demographics ten years from now*; or *conduct a market analysis for trends and changes in customer requirements.*

The facilitator then reads the second target question and another round of slip writing begins. This is repeated for each target question listed. Approximately 10 minutes of writing are allotted for each target. The facilitator can expect about one idea per person per minute of writing time. Following is a list of recommended criteria to use when writing ideas on slips.

- Write until time is called.

- Write for those outside your field.

- Use short sentences and simple words.

- Avoid words like "it" or "this."

- Use a new slip for each response.

- Use only one sentence per slip.

- Start at the very top edge of each slip.

- Write lengthwise on the slip rather than crosswise. (Crawford and Demidovich 1983)

At the completion of the slip writing, all slips are collected from writers and placed in a holding container such as an office in-basket, department store shirt box, or similar container of appropriate size for storing and transporting to the sorting area.

Step 4: Sort the Slips and Determine Major Themes

Sorting is done on a large flat surface such as a library table or small conference table. The facilitator, with the aid of an assistant, sorts out the slips by clustering slips that appear to be directly related to each other. As each slip is drawn from the box, it is reviewed and placed on the table either in an exist-

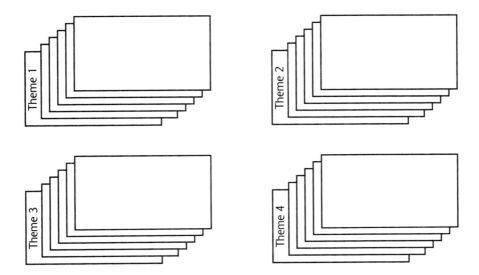

Figure 7-3. Sorting slips by themes.

ing cluster of similar ideas or alone to begin a new cluster. As the slips accumulate in piles, each pile is examined for an appropriate theme represented by the responses. As each theme is determined, it is written on a *classification card* that is placed on the bottom of the pile with the theme clearly visible. Classification cards are prepared earlier by cutting card stock to 3″ by 4¼″ or by using 3″ by 5″ cards if desired. These cards are used to separate the slips by themes. See Figure 7-3 for arrangement of slips and classification cards.

Classification themes may be arranged alphabetically during the sorting procedure for easier identification. Probable themes that may be identified from the example targets provided earlier are *leadership, finances, training, goal setting, communications, process management*, and *customer demographics*. The activities conducted so far are very similar to the Affinity Process except that the themes (headers) are determined by a one- to three-person group rather than the participants as a whole. The themes evolved during the sorting procedure are presented to the team. If a more detailed analysis of responses to target questions is desired, the facilitator may request a rotation procedure where members are asked to respond to any subthemes that were identified by the slips written in the first workshop. Rotation may be performed on all of the themes if necessary.

When the primary classification procedure is completed, the facilitator or team leader will review all slips and themes once again to decide whether there is a need to combine, expand, or make adjustments in the classifications. At this time, *guide cards* are inserted between each pack of slips and classification cards. Guide cards are slightly larger than the classification cards to allow for space to identify the organizational pattern of the themes. For example, the themes may be arranged alphabetically, by prioritization, by sequence, or by some other pattern.

Step 5: Develop the Action Plan

The next step is to develop the action report and plan. This is an action-oriented summary report that describes recommendations related to the target responses. The report is written in a prescriptive rather than descriptive format with the purpose of identifying tasks to be accomplished and how to accomplish them. Dissemination of this report depends upon the targets and previously arranged plans.

For example, suppose the following information were generated so far:

Need: Preparing the organization for the next decade
Target: How to forecast a 10-year vision
Ancillary targets:

- How to analyze future customer and market trends

- How to maintain continuous improvement in the organization's processes and infrastructure

- How to motivate personnel to change to meet future work requirements

Themes identified from the slips:

- leadership

- finances

- training

- goal setting

- communications

- process management

- customer demographics

Main Target—How to forecast a 10-year vision

● = High Impact
○ = Moderate Impact
△ = Low Impact

	Leadership	Finances	Training	Goal Setting	Communications	Process Management	Customer Demographics
Motivate personnel change	● 1	○ 2	● 3	○ 4	● 5	△ 6	△ 7
Analyze future customer-market trends	○ 8	△ 9	△ 10	● 11	● 12	○ 13	● 14
Maintain continuous improvement	● 15	○ 16	○ 17	○ 18	● 19	● 20	○ 21
Adapt new technology	● 22	● 23	● 24	○ 25	○ 26	△ 27	△ 28

Figure 7-4. Simple interaction matrix.

An interaction matrix may be used to present a summary of the impact of these themes on the targets. This then allows the user to make specific recommendations for actions to be taken by the organization. Figure 7-4 suggests use of a simple matrix to identify those interactive points between the themes and ancillary targets. Each cell in the matrix is numbered for clarity and is given an impact measure ranging from high to low impact. The symbols ● (high); ○ (medium); and △ (low) come from the Japanese and are often used to show variation in impact. The writers can quickly see where organization action should be taken by keying in on those cells with ●, indicating high impact, and present specific recommendations for these actions.

The action report provides responses to the four ancillary targets. The summative response to the ancillary targets will answer the main target question by proposing a 10-year vision statement. The result is a prescriptive narration of a vision similar to a scenario. See Figure 7-5 for a sample action plan format.

Action Tasks	Person Responsible	Time Required for Completion	Amount/Source of Funds	Appropriate Personnel	Technology and Facilities	Means of Assessment
1.						
2.						
3.						
4.						
5.						
6.						
7.						
8.						
9.						
10.						
11.						
12.						

Figure 7-5. Action plan matrix.

Step 6: Implement the Action Plan

The final step in the procedure is to implement the action plan and evaluate its effectiveness. This requires the development of assessment instruments and techniques to collect data on the action recommendations produced. Once the data is collected and organized, evaluative decisions may be made that will result in meeting the need expressed earlier. During the evaluation, additional needs will likely be identified, which iterates the process. The CSM model reflects a cyclic process directed at continuous improvement of the organization. In this respect, the CSM model is similar to the Plan, Do, Study, Act sequence more commonly known as the Deming Cycle.

CSM draws upon people within the organization to solve problems and maintain continuous improvement. The challenge to CSM leaders is to prevent stereotypical thinking by team members through direct involvement in the process. An advantage of the individualized creative thinking in CSM is an ability to avoid the phenomenon called "group think," which tends to be more prominent in verbal brainstorming sessions.

The Crawford Slip Method can creatively generate a vision for an organization. The method also extends further, developing assessment procedures that collect data on progress toward the vision as well as additional problems that are manifested during the process.

CSM has been used by a wide variety of organizations including educational institutions, health care providers, city and national governments, dentistry, churches, police and fire departments, the military, and various industries. The method has a long trail of success stories that lend credibility to its process.

What Are Variations of this Tool?

The Crawford Slip Method is somewhat unique in its procedure. It most closely resembles the Affinity Process, whereby creative ideas are solicited from individuals and then processed by a team. The structured format of the CSM offers a more systematic approach to achieving results than do most creative procedures. Variation in the tool may be made at any point in the procedure to accommodate changes in data or the procedure itself.

References

Crawford, C., J. Demidovich, and R. Krone. July 1984. *Productivity Improvement by the Crawford Slip Method*. Los Angeles: University of Southern California School of Public Administration.

Demidovich, J. M. January 1983. *Crawford Slip Method: Brainpower by Think Tank Technology*. Los Angeles: University of Southern California School of Public Administration.

Dettmer, J., R. Krone, and J. Gould. 1989. *Brainpower Networking in Support of TQM Implementation*. A paper presented at the first National Total Quality Management Symposium in Denver, Colorado, November 3.

Chapter 8

Scenario Planning

S cenario Planning is a popular method for determining the possible futures of an organization and is probably the most widely used futuring tool today. The scenarios produced in Scenario Planning are story descriptions of what could happen in an organization's future, based on certain known and unknown factors. They also offer hypothetical sequences of events that allow the planner to identify processes and decision points to construct a more desirable future for the organization.

What Is Its Purpose?

Paul Schoemaker describes scenarios as a structured method of imagining possible futures that organizations can apply to a large number of issues (Schoemaker 1995). Scenario Planning is an effective futuring tool that enables planners to look at what is likely and what is unlikely, knowing quite well that the unlikely elements in an organization are the elements that can determine its relative success. It is valuable in understanding an organization's direction rather than in trying to predict it.

There are many uncertainties facing educational planners currently, such as What is on the horizon for funding in education? What will the condition of the family structure be? and What effect will technology have on education? By utilizing Scenario Planning and by developing three or four probable scenarios, educational planners can develop short- and long-range plans based on the unfolding of the futures in each scenario.

What Is Its Definition?

Herman Kahn, while on the staff of the Rand Corporation and working for the Air Force in the 1960s, was the first to use the term *scenario* in relation to planning in an organization. His definition of a *scenario* is "a hypothetical sequence of events constructed for the purpose of focusing attention on causal events and decision points" (Kahn and Wiener 1967). The process of using scenarios was later expanded by Pierre Wack in his role as a planner for Royal Dutch/Shell (Schwartz 1996). His work was to look for events that might affect the price of oil in the future. Rather than building one probable future, Wack's technique was to develop several scenarios, each of them possible, depending on conditions in the world as played out in the specific scenario. More recently, Peter Schwartz, a member of Global Business Network, defines Scenario Planning as a "tool for ordering one's perception about alternative future environments in which one's decisions might be played out" (Schwartz 1996).

Scenario Planning, then, is defined as a process for developing stories or likely series of events that provide probable futures, with a focus on predetermined and uncertain environments for the purpose of decision making. Scenario Planning is currently being used extensively in management and fits well into current planning, due to the uncertainty of circumstances in business, organizations, and the world in general. Trying to predict what will occur in today's world is speculative at best. Yet we all need to be prepared for the future. Scenario Planning can help.

What Are Its Operational Characteristics?

Scenario Planning has several operational characteristics that enable the planner to fit this tool into the needs of the organization. These are explained in the following list, and are important to study to understand the use and idiosyncrasies of the Scenario Planning tool.

1. Realizes Multiple Futures. If we review the present from the perspective of the past, how often were we right on target with our predictions? Scenario Planning is for those planners who realize that though the future is unpredictable, research and brainpower can narrow down the possibilities to an important few. Scenario Planning takes you into the future with a set of alternative futures, not just one.

2. Ensures Limited Futures. While "multiple futures" are an important characteristic, so are "limited futures." Planning becomes too complicated and unwieldy if the contingencies we plan for are too numerous. Scenario Planning works best when the results are narrowed down to a limited number. Most scenario planners use three or four as the ideal; however, there are exceptions.

3. Considers Environments. The internal and external environments that impact an organization need to be considered in developing alternative futures. These environments are often categorized under the following headings: political, economic, social, technological, legal, environmental, and other factors specific to a school, district, or business.

4. Tells Motivating Stories. Stories have been effective motivators for countless years. In Scenario Planning, this is also the case. Well-written, well-developed, and exciting stories can create enthusiasm for the team and the organization in their planning efforts.

5. Is Creative. The unbounded idealism of creativity is essential for the success of the Scenario Planning process. If we knew where we were headed in the future, we wouldn't need to plan. However, the numerous contingencies possible in taking an organization into the future require the unharnessed creativity of the Scenario Planning team to ensure the future is entered with meaning and purpose.

6. Considers Certainties. While there are many future events and outcomes that we cannot predict with certainty, there are many others that we can "bet on." These certain factors, or predetermined factors, will occur with the highest likelihood no matter what scenario we choose. An example of this is the explosion of technology or the increasing cultural diversity in our society.

7. Considers Uncertainties. What distinguishes scenarios best are the uncertainties. With no uncertainties, we could tell *one* story of our future, with several possible minor variations. With uncertainties the stories take on significantly different outcomes.

8. Focuses on a Problem. Like most problem-solving processes, the results of Scenario Planning are beneficial when the right question is asked or the best issues are defined. While the team is encouraged to be creative on numerous occasions during the process, the initial task of focusing on the most important issue or theme is critical.

What Is Its Structure?

A scenario is a story of a probable future of an organization. The Scenario Planning technique uses at least three but usually not more than four scenarios. Each of the scenarios is developed from certain or predetermined conditions, and from uncertain conditions or *uncertainties*. Figure 8-1 shows a model of Scenario Planning with the four panels illustrating their common

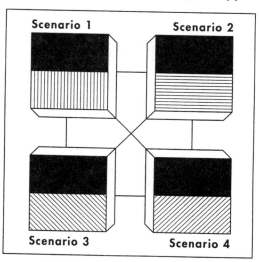

Figure 8-1. The Scenario Planning model.

parts (predetermined conditions) and uncommon parts (uncertain conditions).

What Are Examples of Its Use?

To understand Scenario Planning, we can take a look at an example in our personal lives. Consider a family's vacation plans to whitewater raft in Colorado. The travel agent can provide the necessary brochures, maps, and housing arrangements, which are the known elements or *certainties* for the trip. Scenario Planning can ensure a successful trip by looking at a limited number of possible outcomes. Each of these outcomes, or scenarios, tells a story of what might occur under uncertain conditions, called uncertainties. These could include the weather, the river's water flow, or the camping conditions. The more research that one conducts on the uncertainties, the greater the likelihood that uncertainties can become certainties, thereby enabling one to plan a trip more accurately. For example, if you were to determine the water flow rate down the Colorado River at this time of the year, then the type of clothing needed can be more easily defined, and become a certainty. Likewise, if the camping conditions are well known, they might become a certainty also. Perhaps the only uncertainty left is the weather; however, careful planning might bring up several other uncertainties.

An example of a scenario project was conducted by the National Education Association (NEA) and Global Business Network (GBN) (GBN/NEA 1994). The purpose of the project was to develop a set of scenarios for the future delivery of public education in the United States. The project began in March of that year and was attended by members of the NEA and the GBN staff. Over the course of the next eight months, members of the two organizations met and developed four scenario narratives. In developing these four scenarios, the project made special consideration to three predetermined elements: (1) the decline of the nuclear family, (2) the problem of special education, and (3) the use of technology.

The four scenarios were developed from a matrix based on the following contrasting uncertainties: Will communities of the future be inclusive or exclusive? Will decision making be hierarchical or participatory? Figure 8-2 illustrates the contrasting uncertainties.

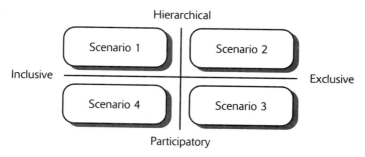

Figure 8-2. Contrasting uncertainties in the GBN/NEA Scenario Project.

The first scenario was titled "The Hierarchical Inclusive Scenario," and it assumes a movement toward traditional values with educators imposing their values on the community. A National Education System is then developed with federal control and a national curriculum.

The second scenario, entitled "The Hierarchical Exclusive Scenario," describes the reaction against a value-free public education. The diverse society calls for public education to avoid imposing any one set of values in order to avoid offending other sets of values. Schools, as the center of the community, reflect the different values that guide different schools.

The third scenario, entitled "The Participatory Exclusive Scenario," is developed around new applications of information technology. The use of information technology is more rapid and far-reaching than expected. Technology will greatly influence education at an accelerated rate so that information technology becomes the biggest story in the transformation of education.

The fourth scenario, entitled "The Participatory Inclusive Scenario," views technology as a significant change agent, making this a radical change scenario; however, the technology serves the ideals of an inclusive community by facilitating a more participatory community. Technology, therefore, is a tool, not a driver, and it serves the interest of play as well as work. It is designed to enhance humanity rather than to make money.

These four scenarios represented the output from several sessions in Scenario Planning. Once the scenarios were completed, the work began; the organization needed to consider the implications of the four scenarios simultaneously as it moved into the future. The analysis of these scenarios revealed many interesting results that could affect the future professional development efforts for the NEA. Three implications were identified by the NEA/GBN team:

1. The Role of Values in Education. The four scenarios sent a message to the team that "values" need to be considered in our educational systems. It was noted that knowing specifically what values to deal with was inconclusive; however, it was clear that some values are better than no values.

2. Information Technology. Teachers cannot afford any longer to remain technologically illiterate. After a decade of humorous discussions about students knowing more about computers than their teachers, the humor needs to be replaced with knowledge. Information must be an integral part of education now.

3. Bridge-building. The world is moving too fast and change is constant. These are givens. Teachers cannot be expected to be in only the classroom. This was acceptable in the past, but is unacceptable now and in the future. Their importance extends to the school community as a collaborative partner.

This example of Scenario Planning is certainly a "big picture" look at education in the United States. Similar planning can be developed for districts, schools, departments, or individuals.

What Is Its Process?

The following steps are used in developing a set of scenarios for organizational future planning.

Step 1: Select the Right Team

It is important that the development of the scenarios in the Scenario Planning process be done by people who are part of the organization as well as by people outside the organization who are major stakeholders or customers. This should include individuals who have the knowledge, interest, and enthusiasm to work for a better organization. In this way, employees can be part of the process and feel ownership for the decisions, and the needed outside

Scenario Planning	
Step 1:	Select the Right Team
Step 2:	Identify the Main Issue to Resolve
Step 3:	List the Key Factors in the Environment
Step 4:	Rank Key Factors
Step 5:	Determine Axes of Uncertainty
Step 6:	Develop Scenarios
Step 7:	Analyze and Interpret Scenarios

Figure 8-3. Steps in Scenario Planning.

information and relationships can be developed. Once the team is formed, it can proceed to Step 2.

Some disadvantages of Scenario Planning evident in this step are: difficulties in (1) obtaining agreement, especially if the focus or themes are controversial; (2) deciding on what scenarios to include; and (3) making certain that the organization and the stakeholders realize that scenarios are not firm predictions. These disadvantages should be taken into consideration when the team is selected.

Step 2: Identify the Main Issue to Resolve

The next step in the process is for the selected team to identify the main issue, focus, or theme of the Scenario Planning process, if the team is empowered to do this. Otherwise, the team may be given this direction by the superintendent, board, or other directing agency. Keep in mind that this process is designed to clarify strategic decisions that will be made by the organization; that is, what is the best decision the team needs to make based on their scenarios. Thus the team is not trying to describe a single or specific future for an organization. Rather, the team is identifying several possible scenarios. This is the reason why Scenario Planning has become such an effective process.

The main issue can be stated in broad terms, such as "What will the future of our school district be in ten years?" Or it can be approached, more

Should we build an additional elementary school?
What outcomes should we identify for our students upon graduation?
Should I change jobs?
Should we invest in a new central computer?
What is the direction of educational funding going to be?
Will the proliferation of VCRs destroy the local movie theaters?
What will be the likely future of media centers vis-a-vis technology?
Should we implement a new discipline policy?

Figure 8-4. Examples of Scenario Planning main issue questions.

specifically, as "How should we develop our curriculum technology plan for the elementary schools?" Defining a good main issue is important to the process. It will provide the motivation for the team and identify the process as worthwhile. Several examples of main issues identified in Scenario Planning processes are listed in Figure 8-4.

Step 3: List the Key Factors in the Environment

Once the main issue is determined, the next step is to identify the major factors, trends, themes, or forces in your specific environment that will influence your organization, relative to that main issue. Just as in any problem-solving process, how the team phrases the question is critical. The team should ask the following question:

What are the major factors we need to know about our future environment in order to make the best decision about _____? (Fill in the main issue, focus, or theme.)

This step is essentially a brainstorming exercise to identify the key factors. A list of 10 to 15 factors is usually sufficient. These generally fall into the categories of political, social, technological, and economic factors, although others, such as environmental, legal, or industry-specific factors may also be

Categories	Considerations/Questions to Ask
Political	Consider elections, regulations, and legislation
	• What will be the makeup of the Board of Education? A supportive or nonsupportive board? • Will new legislation affect the decisions to be made, such as in special education or national standards?
Social	Consider demographics, lifestyles, and values
	• What will the enrollment be in ten years? • What will the family structure be like? • Will values revert to traditional or nontraditional?
Technological	Consider availability, extension, and impact.
	• Will technology significantly change the face of education in its content and delivery?
Economic	Consider financial support, partnerships, and costs
	• Will educational alternatives considerably affect us?

Figure 8-5. List of categories and questions.

considered. Figure 8-5 provides several examples of categories and questions to ask.

Do not be concerned about the importance of each factor as you complete this step. List as many as you can. A sample list responding to two issues—"In light of our increasing population, should we build another elementary school?" and "How can we raise High School Proficiency Test (HSPT) scores?"—is shown in Figure 8-6 and Figure 8-7.

Step 4: Rank Key Factors

Once the list is completed, each entry should be discussed as to how and why it exerts influence on the organization. While we cannot know the future exactly, the team needs to develop a "best guess" discussion. Following the discussion on each factor the team should rank each factor according to its *importance* and *uncertainty*. Figure 8-8 shows the two extremes of *impor-*

• building codes	• housing starts
• available funding	• bond referendum
• community support	• environmental impact
• student demographics	• Board support
• location of building	• ties to long-range plan
• increased staff	• others

Figure 8-6. What are the major factors we need to know about our future environment in order to make our decision about building another elementary school?

tance and *uncertainty*. The outcome of this exercise is to place each of the factors in one of the quadrants in Figure 8-9.

To determine the *importance* of each factor (based on the discussion) answer the questions, "How will this factor impact the organization?" or "How important is this factor?" and then rate each factor as either high or low. Similarly, to determine *uncertainty* (based on the discussion), answer the question, "How uncertain are we that this factor will impact the organization?" Rate each factor as either high or low.

This step is especially significant since it will allow the team to think through each influence factor. The decision on whether a factor is important and what degree of uncertainty it represents will depend on the amount of agreement from the team. A consensus process needs to be used to gain a suitable rating. If the team cannot obtain agreement, then the factor would

• socioeconomic trends	• housing starts
• available funding	• bond referendum
• community support	• environmental impact
• student demographic	• Board support
• readiness for school	• ties to long-range plan
• increased staff	• others

Figure 8-7. What are the major factors we need to know about our future environment in order to make our decision about raising HSPT scores?

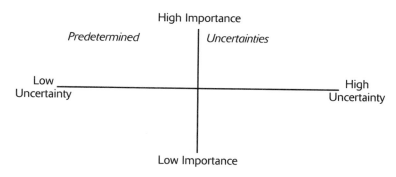

Figure 8-8. Importance—uncertainty quadrants.

most likely be labeled with high uncertainty. For example, the number of twelfth grade students in a school in five years is somewhat predetermined by the number of students in the feeding elementary schools today. This would be labeled high importance/low uncertainty. The political influence wielded by the Board of Education may be labeled as high importance/high uncertainty.

As a result of this sorting, the team can focus their attention on the high importance factors, whether low uncertain or high uncertain. High importance/low uncertainty factors will henceforth be known as *predetermined* factors. High importance/high uncertainty factors will be known simply as *uncertainties*.

The team can ignore all of the factors labeled as low importance/high uncertain or low importance/low uncertain, since they will have little influence on the organization's planning for the future. However, what one team member considers a major factor during a brainstorming session may change when the rating exercise of high or low importance or uncertainty is conducted.

High importance/high uncertainty factors, or simply uncertainties, are the major items that will be used by the scenario writers to shape the various scenarios. High importance/low uncertainty, or simply predetermined factors, will and should be used in all scenarios written, and will be an integral part of the planning process. Scenarios will not differ significantly over predetermined factors, except for how the uncertainties influence these factors.

A list now needs to be developed that ranks the predetermined factors and the uncertainties. This exercise is necessary since it would be relatively impossible to write scenarios that take into account every environmental fac-

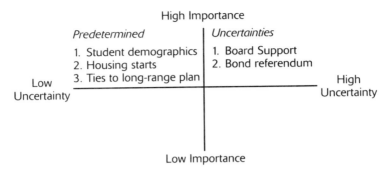

Figure 8-9. List of predetermined and uncertain factors.

tor. This must be a team decision, however. If the length of the list of predetermined factors is relatively short, the team could choose to include them all. Figure 8-9 shows the major factors from the exercise dealing with "building an elementary school" in the importance/uncertainty matrix, listing the factors in priority order.

The team will then look closely at the uncertainties, those high importance/high uncertainty factors. This is the next critical step in the Scenario Planning process.

Step 5: Determine Axes of Uncertainty

One or two uncertainties should be filtered out of this process. These will make up what are known as the *axes of uncertainty*. The axes will represent opposite views of the factors identified as uncertainties. A strong attempt should be made by the team to settle on no more than two axes of uncertainty. If this cannot occur, several conclusions could be drawn: the Scenario Process is not the proper futuring tool; the team should keep on working to narrow down the uncertainties that is—select what is most important; the team should consider writing a bunch of scenarios. One axis of uncertainty will yield no more than two scenarios. Two axes of uncertainty will yield no more than four, while three axes of uncertainty could yield eight scenarios. One possibility to consider when three axes of uncertainty are selected is to identify the eight options but eliminate several based on a discussion with the team. Examples of opposing views in an axis of uncertainty are listed in Figure 8-10.

One view (axis)	Opposing view (axis)
privatization of education	education as a public-sector responsibility
high level of employment	low level of employment
fragmented society	stable society
strong Board of Education support	weak Board of Education support
bond referendum passed	bond referendum failed

Figure 8-10. Examples of labeling opposing views on the axes of uncertainty.

Step 6: Develop Scenarios

Now that the predetermined factors have been selected and the axes of uncertainty have been set, it is time for the team to begin to write the scenarios. Several important features need to be considered in writing scenarios. They are as follows:

1. There should be compelling story lines. Scenarios are not descriptions of the future; rather, they are narratives of how events might unfold between now and then, given the axes of uncertainty that have been assigned to that particular scenario. These story lines should be dramatic, compelling, logical, and plausible.

2. The names of each scenario should be highly descriptive. The name of each one should convey the substance of that scenario. After people have read the story lines, the names should enable them to remember and follow the story.

3. The predetermined factors should be consistent with the selected time frame. For example, if demographics is a predetermined factor, then research must be conducted to ensure that enrollment predictions, for example, are followed.

4. Uncertainty factors should be consistent. For example, full employment and zero inflation do not go together. In this case, that scenario need not be written.

Scenarios are written by returning to the lists of predetermined factors. Each factor should be given some attention in each scenario. In fact, the

Four Scenario Outlines for Building an Elementary School

Scenario 1: Support all around	Scenario 2: Board support with no funding
Predetermined	*Predetermined*
1. Student demographics 2. Housing starts 3. Ties to long-range plan	1. Student demographics 2. Housing starts 3. Ties to long-range plan
Uncertainties	*Uncertainties*
1. High Board support 2. Bond referendum passes	1. High Board support 2. Bond referendum failed
Scenario 3: Funding without Board support	Scenario 4: No funds, no support
Predetermined	*Predetermined*
1. Student demographics 2. Housing starts 3. Ties to long-range plan	1. Student demographics 2. Housing starts 3. Ties to long-range plan
Uncertainties	*Uncertainties*
1. Low Board support 2. Bond referendum passed	1. Low Board support 2. Bond referendum failed

Figure 8-11. List of factors to be considered in writing scenarios for "building an elementary school."

influence and description of the predetermined factors should be relatively the same in each scenario, except for the influence that the uncertainties have on them. Figure 8-11 lists the factors that are to be considered in each scenario from the example of "building an elementary school."

Scenario 1 is written knowing the following certainties: that student demographics were well researched; that the number of housing starts in the township have been identified and know the approximate number of students per unit; and that a long-range plan was developed with new building in mind. Included in Scenario 1 is the fact that there is a high degree of Board support for this concept and that the bond referendum passed, providing the needed funding. This is the most exciting alternative scenario and may be called "Alice in Wonderland" or "Made to Order."

Step 7: Interpretation of Scenarios

Once the scenarios are written, the most important part of the scenario planning process begins: that of determining the implications of each scenario on the main issue, focus, or theme that the team brainstormed in Step 2. One method is to look at the main opportunities and threats identified in each scenario. The team should evaluate each opportunity and threat by determining the capability of the organization to deal with each opportunity and with each threat. Is the organization prepared for the new opportunities identified within each scenario? If not, can it become prepared? How can the organization minimize the threats identified in each scenario?

Another method is to include a table of comparative descriptions on all the scenarios. These tables will help planners and decision-makers see how the scenarios differ within given categories (for example, student body demographics, available funding, business-education partnerships). The dimensions are determined by the team and are used in periodic monitoring of the Scenario Action Plan.

What Are Variations of this Tool?

Several variations to Scenario Planning exist and can prove helpful. The scenario building process in itself is a helpful exercise in developing a vision for an organization. Rather than dealing with uncertainties, the planner can choose the outcome that the organization prefers to move forward, calling it the preferred future. All of the other steps remain relatively intact, with the exception that one scenario is developed and becomes the vision.

One school district reported having developed forty-three possible scenarios. Their process was to develop all possible futures and then choose one that they like best. What they were doing was choosing a most likely future by putting all the marbles in one bag. As of this writing, they have still not been able to come to consensus on the best scenario.

References

Global Business Network and the National Education Associations Scenario Project. 1994. Internet: www.GBN.ORG/SCENARIOS/NEA/NEA.HTML

Kahn, H., and A. J. Weiner. 1967. *The Year 2000: A Framework for Speculation on the Next Thirty-Three Years.* New York: Macmillan.

Schoemaker, P. J. H. 1995. "Scenario Planning: A Tool for Strategic Thinking." *Sloan Management Review* (winter).

Schwartz, P. 1995. *The Art of the Long View.* New York: Doubleday Currency.

Chapter 9

Cross-Impact Analysis

The Cross-Impact Analysis technique was developed by Theodore J. Gordon and Olaf Helmer in 1968. These two men were forecasters who, in reflecting on previous experience, discovered that projected future events are rarely discrete. They found that events are usually interrelated (Hencley and Yates 1974). They observed that the majority of forecasts were event-specific and ignored the potential relationships between and among the future events, and that these interrelationships may very well have significant influence on each other and therefore, the final forecast. Their interest turned toward the development of a technique to examine the rational links or relationships among proposed future events that may then be questioned, modified, or changed in some way based upon the interstimulation and influence each may impose on another. It was believed that if these interrelationships among the events could be determined, the future forecast would become more realistic and perhaps more accurate in its prognosis.

What Is Its Purpose?

The Cross-Impact Analysis is a useful tool for revealing interrelationships or patterns of relationships among projected events and for calculating revised probabilities that are obtained or estimated from the impact of cumulative

130

pair relationships on the projected events. The resulting information is particularly useful for long-range organizational planning.

The events may come from other forecast-producing tools or be generated by a team assigned the responsibility for forecasting the organization's future. In this case, proposed future events are carefully screened and prioritized through consensus and are presented as an *event set*.

The interrelationships impacting on these events are typically *time*, the sequential influence of one event on another as well as the time period selected; *effect*, a measure of whether the influence is positive or negative, enhancing or inhibiting, or necessary for the next event to occur; and *intensity*, the strength of the influence.

What Is Its Definition?

The Cross-Impact Analysis (CIA) is a technique used to identify and analyze the interdependence among selected future events. It employs probability to communicate the likelihood that certain events will exert influence or be influenced, positively or negatively, by other events and to approximate the cumulative impact this has on the final forecast.

What Are Its Operational Characteristics?

The Cross-Impact Analysis tool has certain distinct characteristics that make it different from the other futuring tools presented in this book. The most important characteristics are:

1. Uses a matrix for analysis. The cross-impact is determined by a matrix in which the elements of a forecast or vision are critically examined for their influence and interstimulation of each other. The matrix facilitates the examination of challenges facing the vision and their impact, thereby reaching beyond vision to the strategic future.

2. Analyzes interrelationships. The tool takes a forecast or vision statement and performs a cross-examination of interrelationships among the events, activities, or other phenomena inherent or implied in the vision, in order to understand the challenges facing the vision. The concern is what might occur once the vision is established. The

assumption is that the vision structure will be continuously challenged until the future state is reached.

3. Quantifies results. The tool employs probability as a means of quantifying results. A percentage score is assigned to each event or activity as the vision is developed, indicating the probability of that event or activity occurring as the vision is stated. A revised probability score is given following the matrix analysis of each of the events and activities. The changes are calculated mathematically by computer, which provides feedback on the extent to which the organization can expect its vision to be achieved.

4. May be computerized. The matrix analysis lends itself well to being computerized, allowing the planning team to consider more elements than would be feasible if the analysis were done by hand.

5. Serves as intercessor for other tools. The Cross-Impact Analysis tool takes visions developed by other futuring tools and processes, analyzes them, and feeds the results into the Futuring Tree for implementation. It may, therefore, be viewed as an intercessor that can convert a vision to a strategic quality future.

What Is Its Structure?

The Cross-Impact Analysis uses a matrix to conduct the analysis of interrelationships of events. An event set (E1, E2, E3, and so on) ranging from as few as five to about twenty events are listed vertically on the y axis in the matrix. (Some applications have used as many as 40 events for an analysis done on a computer.) The probability of each event occurring is then estimated. The same events are also listed horizontally on the x axis. Each event pair, beginning with E1 on the y axis and E2 on the x axis, is analyzed for relationships and is given a conditional probability based upon the nature and strength of the influence. The revised probabilities are then used in the final forecast. See matrix structure in Figure 9-1.

Cross-Impact Analysis—Event Matrix

The effect on this event is . . .

If this event occurs—	E1	E2	E3	E4	E5
E1	■				
E2		■			
E3			■		
E4				■	
E5					■

Figure 9-1. Cross-Impact Analysis matrix model.

What Are Examples of Its Use?

The Cross-Impact Analysis tool has been used in a variety of situations to examine relationships between and among such variables as air pollution, mass transit, energy crises, taxation, birthrate, and many others. For example, realizing that widespread use of mass-produced electric-powered automobiles would be likely to have an impact on the above variables, an event matrix was used to conduct an analysis of the interrelationships that can occur and their consequences. Timing of the introduction of the electric car was influenced by the results of this analysis.

Other areas in which Cross-Impact Analysis is used to analyze cause-effect relationships are in the development of new technology, innovation, demographic changes, career selection, social issues and problems, and military activities.

The tool is particularly useful for detecting errors or inconsistencies in projected future events as well as in advertised claims or promises of predicted future events.

Cross-Impact Analysis	
Step 1:	Assemble the Appropriate Team
Step 2:	Identify the Events to Be Used in the Analysis
Step 3:	Place the Event Set on the *y* Axis of the Matrix
Step 4:	Complete the *x* Axis of the Matrix
Step 5:	Analyze the Relationships among Events and Estimate their Impact for Each Event Pair
Step 6:	Calculate Totals for Columns and Rows
Step 7:	Summarize the Results of the Analysis

Figure 9-2. Steps in developing a Cross-Impact Analysis.

What Is Its Process?

Since its creation, there have been several variations developed in the Cross-Impact Analysis technique, ranging from simple to rather complex analyses. Selection of the analysis procedure is determined by the end results desired. For example, you may wish to examine linkages among the events to determine only whether they are enhancing or inhibiting relationships, or perhaps to discover that they are unrelated. These linkages would appear in a simple matrix using positive numbers, negative numbers, or 0 to indicate no effect as shown in Figure 9-3. The procedure for developing this matrix is as follows.

Step 1: Assemble the Appropriate Team

An appropriate team in this instance would be a future planning or strategic planning team which has cross-functional membership and is trained in futuring techniques. The procedure is to collect general research information about what the future may be like ten years from now by reviewing projected changes in those social-cultural, economic, political, and technical arenas related to the organization. Following this review, a list of proposed future events that could directly impact the organization may be identified by the team. The list is screened for duplication or obvious gaps and may be

The effect on this event is . . .

If this event occurs—	E1	E2	E3	E4	E5
E1 Event		+1	0	0	+1
E2 Event	0		+3	+1	−1
E3 Event	+1	0		+2	−1
E4 Event	0	−1	−1		−3
E5 Event	+1	+2	−1	−1	

Figure 9-3. Matrix showing hypothetical interrelationships among events.

condensed, added to, or refined. This list is then voted upon using the Nominal Group Technique to rank order the events and reach consensus on that order.

Step 2: Identify the Events to Be Used in the Analysis

An event set is a group of five to twenty or more events that are forecast as very likely to occur within a given future time period. These events are expected to have a significant effect on the organization's future and are, therefore, examined by the Cross-Impact Analysis to determine probable interrelationships and their possible impact on the future.

The initial event set may come from a prior forecasting process which presents a list of probable future events that are likely to have an impact on an organization. If this is not available, the organization may develop the event set themselves using an appropriate team and tools. Selection of the number of events for the event set is based on team judgment and knowledge of their significance and location in the ranking, the positive or negative influence created by these events, the enhancing or inhibiting impact, and the intensity of the influence in bringing about change in the relationships.

Considered in the team's judgment of significance are the inherent inter-relationships foreseen among the events, such as the timing or sequencing of

Future Event	Likely Effects
E1 The State Department of Education will require core academic curricula and outcomes standards as well as increased math, science, and technology credits for high school graduation.	This event may reduce competition by bringing all schools to the same levels of academic standards. Student recruitment and enrollments will be enhanced by this.
E2 Competition with public schools, magnet and alternative schools, as well as the newly developing charter schools, will increase.	This competition will affect recruitment and admission of students. It will also have a general negative effect on enrollments and possibly cause tuition increases.
E3 State and federal governments will maintain direct and indirect financial support of private schools.	Maintenance of funds will impact negatively on increased academic standards, competition for students and funds, and test results. This will have a slight positive effect on enrollment management.
E4 Demographic shifts will increase enrollment pools of minorities and recent immigrant families. This may be exacerbated by the voucher system or programs allowing choice for urban students.	This will create increased reading and language instruction, cultural awareness, and adaptability. Largest increases likely to be in Hispanic students followed by Afro-American and Asian students. Perhaps a greater percentage of involvement will emerge. The negative effect on increased testing is based on reading, language, and cultural variations not accounted for in the testing.
E5 Increased testing will be supported by the national concern for core standards and measurable results of the educational process.	Increased testing will highly affect state-imposed academic standards in a reciprocal relationship. Student enrollments should be affected positively by the increased opportunities for feedback on district results of instruction.

Figure 9-4. Sample Future Events for private schools.

each event; the conditional impact; and the strength of the influence one event may have on others. The top five to ten events should provide an acceptable forum for analysis in the Cross-Impact Matrix. An example of five events describing the future of private schools might look like Figure 9-4.

During this step, team members may engage in forms of role playing or debating to present advocacy or difficult ideas concerning the events and their effects.

Step 3: Place the Event Set on the y Axis of the Matrix

The y axis of the matrix shows the list of events predicted to have the highest impact on the organization ten years from now. The events are entered into the matrix in statement form for clarity and are coded as E1, E2, E3, and so on, to facilitate analysis. The y axis carries a standard title—*If this event occurs:*—that is placed at the top of the event list. Figure 9-5 shows an event set of five highly probable future events for a private school district in a suburban section of a metropolitan area. The projected time frame is approximately ten years from now.

The effect on this event is . . .

If this event occurs—		E1	E2	E3	E4	E5	
E1	State-imposed increases on academic requirements for private schools.		−1	0	+3	0	= +2
E2	Increased competition for students and funds in public, magnet, alternative, and charter schools.	−2		0	+3	+1	= +2
E3	State and federal funds maintained. Encourage formation of partnerships for resources.	−1	−2		+1	−1	= −3
E4	Demographic shifts in enrollment management. Increase in minority populations.	0	0	−1		−2	= −3
E5	State increase in diagnostic and achievement testing in grades 1, 4, 8, and 11.	+4	0	−1	+1		= +4
		= +1	= −3	= −2	= +8	= −2	+2

Matrix index = +2

Figure 9-5. Sample Cross-Impact Matrix for a private school district.

Step 4: Complete the x Axis of the Matrix

The horizontal *x* axis is completed by listing the event codes from left to right across the top of the matrix as shown in Figure 9-5. Events on the *x* axis are also coded E1, E2, E3, and so on. Other code factors such as an additional E may be added (for example, EE1) to indicate the effect on the event and to distinguish them from those on the *y* axis, in order to avoid confusion during the pair analysis. They would appear then as EE1, EE2, EE3, and so on. The *x* axis is titled *The effect on this event would be. . . .*

Step 5: Analyze the Relationships among Events and Estimate their Impact for Each Event Pair

To begin, the team focuses on the E1 statement in the left column. Since it is useless to compare E1 with E1 (they are the same), that matrix cell is blocked out. Therefore, the analyst goes to the right to the cell immediately under E2 and asks the question *What is the effect of E1 on E2?* Responses to this question will fall on a continuum such as the one following.

+5	+4	+3	+2	+1	0	−1	−2	−3	−4	−5
High		Enhancing		Low	Unrelated	Low		Inhibiting		High

The team determines the appropriate number and places that number with the + or − sign in the cell. The 0 carries no + or − sign. To facilitate rating the effects, the events should be clarified for team members to be sure they all understand what each event means.

Following the examination of E1 and E2, the team now considers E1 and E3 and asks the same question; that is, What is the effect of E1 on E3? A numerical value is placed in the appropriate cell. This procedure continues with E1 to E4 and E1 to E5. This is considered one cycle. The next cycle begins with a comparison of E2 with E1, E3, E4, and E5 in succession. Although this procedure is repetitive, it needs to be completed carefully to ascertain important relationships or effects among the events.

Step 6: Calculate Totals for Columns and Rows

When the analysis is complete, it is helpful to sum each row and column to arrive at a matrix index that serves as a general indicator of the cumulative effects of the event set.

Using the numbers in Figure 9-5, the sum of the row for E1 (−1, 0, +3, 0) = +2. This number is added to the right edge of the matrix as shown. The remaining rows are summed and their results also posted.

The columns are now summed beginning with E1. The total is +1. The remaining columns are summed and the matrix index is determined, reflecting the sum of the sums in both columns and rows.

Step 7: Summarize the Results of the Analysis

As indicated earlier, the advantage of using the Cross-Impact Analysis is that single events produced by a forecasting procedure can be taken one step further and analyzed for any linkages or interrelationships that exist among them. From this analysis, patterns of chained relationships are revealed, which increases the accuracy of the forecasting process. A sample of these relationships is provided below.

Based on the analysis of the events in Figure 9-5, one might conclude that:

- Student enrollment management is influenced by all other events, indicating relative dependency of enrollment on conditions occurring at the designated time.

- Although increased competition for students and funds may have a negative effect on increased academic standards, there will be positive effects on student enrollment and state testing.

- If the state imposed increased academic requirements, it would result in closer analysis of enrollment management and state testing.

- Increased state testing has the highest impact across the board when compared to the other events.

- State increases in academic standards and competition for students and funds show a moderate positive impact on events across the board.

- Maintaining financial support and student enrollment management indicate across-the-board negative effects that will require much attention during the next ten years.

- The overall matrix index is +2, suggesting that these events present a slightly to moderately enhancing future forecast.

Advanced Matrix Analysis Using Probability

The above example of a Cross-Impact Analysis application was presented in its simplest form to accommodate successful hands-on use by a future planning team. More advanced procedures for CIA involve the use of probability estimation, which provides a mathematical model that may be calculated and analyzed by hand or by computer.

The following example of Cross-Impact Analysis uses probability estimates that are adjusted once the interrelationships of the event set are determined. The probabilities are calculated using the appropriate mathematical formula. The complexity of this procedure is contained so that planning teams can elect to analyze the data by hand, calculator, or by use of a computer.

Step 1 and 2: Using an Appropriate Team, Identify the Events To Be Analyzed

Using the descriptions and procedures for obtaining a projected set of future events as explained in the earlier example, a new event set is selected that focuses on a medium size urban school district. Five events forecast for this situation might look like these.

E1: Student enrollments shift due to implementation of a school voucher system, increased expansion of other types of schools such as magnet and alternative schools and charter schools, and competition from private schools.

E2: A broad implementation of school-to-work transition programs is developed collaboratively through industry and education partnerships.

E3: State and federal funding for urban schools remains relatively stable and proportionate to needs over the next 10-year-period.

E4: Community-controlled schools are formed through site-based management and governed by local advisory groups composed of parents, teachers, administrators, and community stakeholders.

E5: Schools become educational, cultural, and recreational centers in their communities, providing a variety of preschool, afternoon, and evening activities for all community members.

Step 3: Place the Event Set on the y Axis of the Matrix

As in the prior example, the five future events are placed on the y (vertical) axis of the matrix as shown in Figure 9-6. The title, *If this event occurs—* is located over the y axis. An additional column is added for estimates of the initial probability of the events.

			The effect on this event is . . .				
If this event occurs—		Initial Probability	E1	E2	E3	E4	E5
E1	Shifts in enrollments to different schools	0.50	■				
E2	Increased school-to-work programs	0.60		■			
E3	Stable state and federal funding	0.30			■		
E4	Development of community controlled schools	0.20				■	
E5	Schools become community centers	0.40					■

Figure 9-6. Cross-Impact Matrix for urban schools showing initial probabilities.

Step 4: Complete the x Axis of the Matrix

The *x* axis has five columns, one for each of the events. The same five events are listed across the top of the matrix, and are posted as E1, E2, E3, and so on, to identify them during the analysis process. The *x* axis uses the title *The effect on this event is . . .* to properly label the percentage of "conditional probability" developed within the matrix cells.

Step 5: Estimate the Initial Probability for each Event

In this example, each future event is judged for its probability of occurrence within the ten-year time frame projected in the strategic plan. The team must consider each event in the context of all other events and assign an initial probability percentage for each event based upon answers to the following question: *Given the total event set, what is the probability that this event will occur within the next ten years?* Initial probability estimates are placed in the matrix column next to the events. See Figure 9-6. It is important that the team has a cross-functional membership and that members have intuitive abilities to estimate these probabilities as accurately as possible.

Important relationships to look for in the analysis are:

- What is the effect on the probability of one event occurring before, simultaneously with, or after another? For instance, if E1 occurs before E2, would the initial probability be affected? If E1 occurs simultaneously with or after E2, would there be any change in their probabilities?

- The team may discover that one or two of the events have high enhancing influence and may be considered "drivers." With this new knowledge, will the initial probabilities be affected by their interrelationships?

- Once a relationship has been established between events, the team must judge whether the effect of that relationship is positive or negative; that is, enhancing or inhibiting, or null. A relationship might exist between two events but the effect on both events remains essentially neutral or null.

- As in most analyses, the magnitude of the effect one event has on another must be determined to realize the strength of the influence. For example, E2 (broad implementation of school-to-work transition programs) is being driven by national leaders and funded by federal grants. These conditions will likely strengthen the impact of E2 on E1, E3, and E5. The strength of this influence may increase the initial probability of E3 and E5, hence the need to examine the interrelationships and revise their probabilities of occurrence in this context.

Step 6: Calculate the Conditional Probabilities in the Matrix

The team now begins the process of analyzing relationships between and among events to determine the accuracy of the initial probabilities.

The conditional probabilities are those that take into account the interrelationships and influences that might be revealed when one event is compared with another. The mathematical formula takes the initial probabilities and examines the range of impact from highest to lowest and negative to positive, and determines a conditional probability for each event based upon conditions generated by the interrelationships.

Figure 9-6 presents an event set which is forecast for a medium size urban school district. (See Step 1 in this section.) Each event has been given an estimated initial probability based upon the intuitive judgment of the futuring team. The judgment is focused on the probability of each event occurring within the time period hypothesized. The team must now consider the potential impact and influence of each event on each other, taking into account timing, positive or negative impact, and the strength of that impact. This analysis results in a conditional probability for each event based upon these possible interrelationships.

The analysis is conducted the same as in the earlier example, namely, E1 to E2; E1 to E3; E1 to E4; and E1 to E5. The process is repeated with E2 through E5 until each event has been compared with each other event. The number of event-pair interactions to be considered may be calculated as $n^2 - n$ where n equals the number of events. Therefore, $5 \times 5 = 25 - 5 = 20$ interactions.

The first event-pair analysis is to examine the effects on the probability of event E1 (shifts in enrollments) in relation to the probability of E2 (increasing school-to-work programs). The following formula is used to examine these effects:

$$Pe' = KS\ (t - tm)/t\ Pe^2 + (1 - KS\ (t - tm)/t)\ Pe\ \text{(Gordon and Stover 1978)}$$

Where

Pe' = the probability of occurrence of event "A" (E1) at some time after the occurrence of event "B" (E2).

Pe = the probability of occurrence of event "A" (E1) before the occurrence of event "B" (E2).

K = +1 if the impact of event "B" on event "A" is inhibiting, and −1 if the impact is enhancing.

S = the strength of the impact (designated as a number between 0 and 1).

t = the time for which the probabilities are being estimated (10 years).

tm = the time in the future when event "B" will occur.

A sample calculation of the conditional probability for E1/E2 is as follows:

$$Pe' = -1 \times .30 \times ((10 - 3)/10) \times (.2)^2 + ((1 - (-1 \times .30 \times (10 - 3)/10)) \times .20)$$

$$Pe' = -.30 \times (.70) \times .04 + (1 - (-.30 \times (.70)) \times .20)$$

$$Pe' = -.0084 + ((1 - (-.21)) \times .2\ )$$

$$Pe' = -.0084 + (1.21) \times .2\ )$$

$$Pe' = -.0084 + (.242\ )$$

$$Pe' = .2336$$

Values for calculations of the conditional probabilities for the five events in Figure 9-6 are shown in Figure 9-8.

Event Pair	Values	Event Pairs	Values
E1/E2	Pe = .20	E1/E3	Pe = .10
	K = −1		K = −1
	S = .30		S = .50
	t = 10		t = 10
	tm = 3		tm = 2
E1/E4	Pe = .70	E1/E5	Pe = .80
	K = −1		K = −1
	S = .80		S = .10
	t = 10		t = 10
	tm = 10		tm = 5
E2/E1	Pe = .60	E2/E3	Pe = .70
	K = −1		K = −1
	S = .30		S = .50
	t = 10		t = 10
	tm = 8		tm = 2
E2/E4	Pe = .80	E2/E5	Pe = .50
	K = +1		K = −1
	S = .50		S = .30
	t = 10		t = 10
	tm = 10		tm = 5
E3/E1	Pe = .60	E3/E2	Pe = .70
	K = +1		K = −1
	S = .40		S = .50
	t = 10		t = 10
	tm = 8		tm = 3
E3/E4	Pe = .80	E3/E5	Pe = .80
	K = +1		K = −1
	S = .10		S = .30
	t = 10		t = 10
	tm = 10		tm = 5

Figure 9-7. Values for calculating conditional probabilities.

Event Pair	Values	Event Pairs	Values
E4/E1	Pe = .20 K = +1 S = .30 t = 10 tm = 8	E4/E2	Pe = .05 K = −1 S = .30 t = 10 tm = 3
E4/E3	Pe = .01 K = −1 S = .60 t = 10 tm = 2	E4/E5	Pe = .05 K = −1 S = .70 t = 10 tm = 5
E5/E1	Pe = .50 K = +1 S = .30 t = 10 tm = 8	E5/E2	Pe = .50 K = −1 S = .60 t = 10 tm = 3
E5/E3	Pe = .40 K = −1 S = .70 t = 10 tm = 2	E5/E4	Pe = .80 K = −1 S = .90 t = 10 tm = 10

Figure 9-7. (Continued).

Step 7: Examine Matrix Probabilities Using Table of Conditional Probabilities

The conditional probabilities appearing in the matrix cells may be checked for accuracy by calculating the mathematical range of possibility for each cell. For example, the conditional probability for E1 and E2 in Figure 9-8 is 0.2336. The values calculated into the formula represent the best estimates of the team members. To ensure that the values are realistic and reasonably accurate, each conditional probability is compared to mathematically structured ranges of probability based upon standard values entered into the formula. These ranges are determined by the table in Figure 9-9.

If this event occurs—	Initial Probability	The effect on this event is . . .				
		E1	E2	E3	E4	E5
E1 Shifts in enrollments to different schools.	0.50	■	.17 / .83	.00 / 1.0	.00 / 1.0	.00 / 1.0
E2 Increased school-to-work programs	0.60	.20 / 1.0	■	.00 / 1.0	.00 / 1.0	.38 / 1.0
E3 Stable state and federal funding	0.30	.00 / .60	.00 / .50	■	.00 / 1.0	.00 / .75
E4 Development of community controlled schools	0.20	.00 / .40	.00 / .33	.00 / .67	■	.00 / .50
E5 Schools become community centers	0.40	.00 / .80	.00 / .67	.00 / 1.0	.00 / 1.0	■

Figure 9-8. Conditional probabilities for each event pair analysis.

The table probability ranges are based on the following formula:

$$P(1) = P(2) \times P(1/2) + P(\bar{2}) \times P(1/\bar{2})$$

Where:

P(1) = the probability that event 1 (E1) will occur

P(2) = the probability that event 2 (E2) will occur

P(1/2) = the probability of event 1 given the occurrence of event 2

P($\bar{2}$) = the probability that event 2 will not occur

P(1/$\bar{2}$) = the probability of event 1 given the nonoccurrence of event 2

An example: The initial probability for event 1 (E1) is estimated at 0.50. The probability for event 2 (E2) is 0.60. Using the formula, the range of conditional probability is found to be 0.17 to 0.83. This is calculated by rearranging the formula using the following values:

$$P(1/2) = (P(1) - P(\bar{2}) \times P(1/\bar{2}))/P(2)$$

Where:

P(1/2) = the range of probability for E1 given the occurrence of E2

P(1) = the initial probability for E1

If each of these occur

⇕   ⇕   what is the probability of these events?

⇕	E 1 .05	E 2 .10	E 3 .15	E 4 .20	E 5 .25	E 6 .30	E 7 .35	E 8 .40	E 9 .45	E 10 .50	E 11 .55	E 12 .60	E 13 .65	E 14 .70	E 15 .75	E 16 .80	E 17 .85	E 18 .90	E 19 .95
E 1 .05	1.00	1.00	1.00	1.00	1.00	1.00	1.00	1.00	1.00	1.00	1.00	1.00	1.00	1.00	1.00	1.00	1.00	1.00	1.00
	.00	.00	.00	.00	.00	.00	.00	.00	.00	.00	.00	.00	.00	.00	.00	.00	.00	.00	.00
E 2 .10	.05	1.00	1.00	1.00	1.00	1.00	1.00	1.00	1.00	1.00	1.00	1.00	1.00	1.00	1.00	1.00	1.00	1.00	1.00
	.00	.00	.00	.00	.00	.00	.00	.00	.00	.00	.00	.00	.00	.00	.00	.00	.00	.00	.50
E 3 .15	.33	.67	1.00	1.00	1.00	1.00	1.00	1.00	1.00	1.00	1.00	1.00	1.00	1.00	1.00	1.00	1.00	1.00	1.00
	.00	.00	.00	.00	.00	.00	.00	.00	.00	.00	.00	.00	.00	.00	.00	.00	.00	.33	.67
E 4 .20	.25	.50	.75	1.00	1.00	1.00	1.00	1.00	1.00	1.00	1.00	1.00	1.00	1.00	1.00	1.00	1.00	1.00	1.00
	.00	.00	.00	.00	.00	.00	.00	.00	.00	.00	.00	.00	.00	.00	.00	.00	.25	.50	.75
E 5 .25	.20	.40	.60	.80	1.00	1.00	1.00	1.00	1.00	1.00	1.00	1.00	1.00	1.00	1.00	1.00	1.00	1.00	1.00
	.00	.00	.00	.00	.00	.00	.00	.00	.00	.00	.00	.00	.00	.00	.00	.20	.40	.60	.80
E 6 .30	.17	.33	.50	.67	.83	1.00	1.00	1.00	1.00	1.00	1.00	1.00	1.00	1.00	1.00	1.00	1.00	1.00	1.00
	.00	.00	.00	.00	.00	.00	.00	.00	.00	.00	.00	.00	.00	.00	.17	.33	.50	.67	.83
E 7 .35	.14	.29	.43	.57	.71	.85	1.00	1.00	1.00	1.00	1.00	1.00	1.00	1.00	1.00	1.00	1.00	1.00	1.00
	.00	.00	.00	.00	.00	.00	.00	.00	.00	.00	.00	.00	.00	.14	.29	.43	.57	.71	.86
E 8 .40	.13	.25	.38	.50	.62	.75	.87	1.00	1.00	1.00	1.00	1.00	1.00	1.00	1.00	1.00	1.00	1.00	1.00
	.00	.00	.00	.00	.00	.00	.00	.00	.00	.00	.00	.00	.12	.25	.38	.50	.63	.75	.88
E 9 .45	.11	.22	.33	.44	.56	.67	.78	.89	1.00	1.00	1.00	1.00	1.00	1.00	1.00	1.00	1.00	1.00	1.00
	.00	.00	.00	.00	.00	.00	.00	.00	.00	.00	.00	.11	.22	.33	.44	.56	.67	.78	.89
E 10 .50	.10	.20	.30	.40	.50	.60	.70	.80	.90	1.00	1.00	1.00	1.00	1.00	1.00	1.00	1.00	1.00	1.00
	.00	.00	.00	.00	.00	.00	.00	.00	.00	.00	.10	.20	.30	.40	.50	.60	.70	.80	.90
E 11 .55	.09	.18	.27	.36	.45	.55	.64	.73	.82	.91	1.00	1.00	1.00	1.00	1.00	1.00	1.00	1.00	1.00
	.00	.00	.00	.00	.00	.00	.00	.00	.00	.09	.18	.27	.36	.45	.55	.64	.73	.82	.91
E 12 .60	.08	.17	.25	.33	.42	.50	.58	.67	.75	.83	.92	1.00	1.00	1.00	1.00	1.00	1.00	1.00	1.00
	.00	.00	.00	.00	.00	.00	.00	.00	.00	.17	.25	.33	.42	.50	.58	.67	.75	.83	.92
E 13 .65	.08	.15	.23	.31	.38	.46	.54	.62	.69	.77	.85	.92	1.00	1.00	1.00	1.00	1.00	1.00	1.00
	.00	.00	.00	.00	.00	.00	.00	.08	.15	.23	.31	.38	.46	.54	.63	.69	.77	.85	.92
E 14 .70	.07	.14	.21	.29	.36	.43	.50	.57	.64	.71	.79	.86	.93	1.00	1.00	1.00	1.00	1.00	1.00
	.00	.00	.00	.00	.00	.00	.07	.14	.21	.29	.36	.43	.50	.57	.64	.71	.79	.86	.93
E 15 .75	.07	.13	.20	.27	.33	.40	.47	.53	.60	.67	.73	.80	.87	.93	1.00	1.00	1.00	1.00	1.00
	.00	.00	.00	.00	.00	.07	.13	.20	.27	.33	.40	.47	.53	.60	.67	.73	.80	.87	.93
E 16 .80	.06	.13	.19	.25	.31	.38	.44	.50	.56	.62	.69	.75	.81	.87	.94	1.00	1.00	1.00	1.00
	.00	.00	.00	.00	.00	.13	.19	.25	.31	.38	.44	.50	.56	.63	.69	.75	.81	.87	.94
E 17 .85	.00	.12	.18	.24	.29	.35	.41	.47	.53	.59	.65	.71	.78	.82	.88	.94	1.00	1.00	1.00
	.00	.00	.00	.06	.12	.18	.24	.29	.35	.41	.47	.53	.59	.65	.71	.76	.82	.88	.94
E 18 .90	.00	.11	.17	.22	.28	.33	.39	.44	.50	.56	.61	.67	.72	.78	.83	.89	.94	1.00	1.00
	.00	.00	.00	.11	.17	.22	.28	.33	.39	.44	.50	.56	.61	.67	.72	.78	.83	.88	.94
E 19 .95	.00	.11	.16	.21	.26	.32	.37	.42	.47	.53	.58	.63	.68	.74	.79	.84	.89	.95	1.00
	.00	.05	.11	.16	.21	.26	.32	.37	.42	.47	.53	.58	.63	.68	.74	.79	.84	.89	.94

Figure 9-9. Table of limits for conditional probability.

P(2) = the initial probability of E2

P($\bar{2}$) = 1 minus the initial probability of E2

P(1/2) = (unknown)—substitute 0.0 to calculate the highest probability and 1.0 for the lowest probability

Solving for

$$P(1/2) = (.50 - (1 - .60) \times 0.0 \text{ (or } 1.0))/.75$$

$$P(1/2) = (.50 - .40 \times 0.0)/.60 = .50/.60 = .83 \text{ as the highest probability}$$

$$P(1/2) = (.50 - .40 \times 1.0)/.60 = .10/.60 = .17 \text{ as the lowest probability}$$

The range of probability may be determined quickly by using the Table of Limits for Conditional Probabilities shown in Figure 9-9. The table data is arranged in matrix format. To find the highest and lowest probability limits, locate the initial probability for E1 (.50) by moving horizontally across the top of the columns until .50 is located. It happens to be under E10, which is an arbitrary column numbering system and is not related to the matrix you are working with.

Follow the column downward to the intersection of E12 where .60, the initial probability for E2 in the working matrix, is found. The cell where these two values intersect shows a probability range of .17 to .83. This coincides with the formula calculations and confirms that the probability estimates are reasonable and workable. If the probability calculation does not fit into this range, the factors used to determine this calculation need to be reconsidered including the estimated initial probability.

Additional Steps

Other steps are normally pursued when conducting the Cross-Impact Analysis by computer. They are: (1) perform a calibration run of the matrix values by selecting an event for testing and, using a random number, comparing its probability to determine occurrence or nonoccurrence of the event and its impact on all other events.

A follow-up step is to conduct tests for policies, actions, and sensitivity. Impacts are usually calculated by using odds ratios rather than probability formulas. Because of the complex nature of these steps, they are not included in this chapter. The authors feel that the futuring team will be able to handle the information processing described so far and thus be able to obtain the benefits of this tool for critically analyzing an organization's vision or forecast.

Summary

The Cross-Impact Analysis matrix provides a means for taking an initial forecast of future events for an organization and analyzing the relationships each event may have with another. This "second effort" of analyzing relationships of events after they have been selected and forecast is what gives the tool its importance. So often, visions are developed without the rigor of systematic examination and comparison with other possible factors, which tends to weaken the reliability of the vision. This tool goes one step further to examine and cross-examine probable future events for an organization, resulting in a more accurate future forecast.

The Cross-Impact Analysis is widely used by corporations and other organizations for future forecasting. When calculating conditional probabilities of events from their initial probabilities, the computer is used because of the large number of calculations required (usually when dealing with between ten and forty events). This process produces high levels of confidence in the analysis summary.

What Are Variations of this Tool?

A significant variation in this process is in the extended analysis. For instance, the process described so far relies upon analyses of event pairs. The assumption is that adequate data can be collected by examining relationships between event pairs as the basic unit of analysis. Inconsistencies in data that would not be detected by analyzing in pairs may be revealed if the events are examined in triads or quartets. The *calibration test* is used to check the relationships occurring between and among the events by pairs, triplets, quartets, and so on. This requires a computer program designed to compare probabilities with random numbers to determine occurrence or nonoccurrence of events and calculate the impacts on all other events as a result of the occurrence or nonoccurrence. The impacts are normally calculated using odds ratios rather than probabilities, in order to reflect event impacts more sharply.

A test for *nonoccurrence impacts* may be used when analyzing events and comparing them with *occurrence impacts* caused by the relationships between events. These should balance each other.

A *sensitivity test* is used when there may be uncertainty about an initial or conditional probability. This procedure involves altering a selected judged value (probability) and running the matrix probabilities again. If the altered value changes the matrix results, then it may be assumed that an error occurred in the initial judgment. If no significant change occurred, then the judged value is consistent.

Policy testing is another test that involves evaluation of organizational or external policy that might affect the events in the matrix. For example, a sudden change in the school funding formula by the state government may have a significant impact on the event set used in the matrix. Internal changes in the school district, such as the transformation to site-based management, may also affect the event set and require policy testing. The testing is accomplished by first anticipating what policy changes might take place, estimating their possible effects on the event set in the matrix, and developing alternative events that are then processed in a new matrix.

References

Fildes, R. 1987. "Forecasting: The Issues." *The Handbook of Forecasting: A Manager's Guide.* New York: John Wiley & Sons, p.161.

Helmer, O. 1987. "Problems in Futures Research—Delphi and Causal Cross-Impact Analysis" *Futures.* vol. 9, p.71.

Hencley, S. P,. and J. R. Yates. 1974. *Futurism in Education.* Berkeley, CA: McCutcheon Publishing Company, p. 115–126.

Wheelwright, S. C., and S. Makridakis. 1985. *Forecasting Methods for Management.* New York: John Riley & Sons.

Chapter 10

Futuring Tree

The Futuring Tree is a goal-oriented tool that starts with a description of the future state and works backward through a network of alternative pathways to connect an organization's future with its present. The process is much like that of an airline pilot who files a flight plan prior to the journey to show the destination, air routes to be followed, and the navigational check points or "waypoints" along the way. The destination is first located on an aviation chart. The pilot traces the air routes backward toward the departure point to find the most direct and feasible route(s) to follow. The checkpoints are used to track the flight path of the airplane and monitor its progress while en route to its destination.

What Is Its Purpose?

The Futuring Tree procedure allows its users to identify a future goal in the form of a vision or strategic future plan and then reason backward to determine what activities and events must be developed to reach that goal. This is very much like linking an organization's strategic plan with its annual or operational plan. The tool employs a branch point diagram with a complex visual network of alternative pathways that connect an organization's present with its desired future. The network also identifies constraints and critical decision points that may present barriers or prevent organizations from attaining desirable goals. A series of *priority pathways* through the internal network are discovered, which enables the organization to connect more efficiently. Priority pathways are those that provide the most feasible directions through the network. Although many pathways will surface, those that show the best cost benefit analysis and the most efficient use of human and fiscal resources and time, are important to the success of the organization in achieving its future goal.

The Futuring Tree is a powerful management tool for helping organizations reach their preferred future. The tool exercises internal control over its processes, sequence, and hierarchy of events within the network, relationships among these events, and an accounting of the approximate time necessary to navigate the network. It also has built-in checkpoints to monitor the stability of the procedure.

What Is Its Definition?

The Futuring Tree provides a process for connecting an organization's future state with its present state through a network of priority pathways working from the future to the present. The process begins with an analysis of the future state and the development of a branch point diagram that reveals alternatives, constraints, interrelationships, critical decision points, and priority pathways that link elements of the future state with the present state of an organization.

What Are Its Operational Characteristics?

Five characteristics identify the Futuring Tree as a unique tool for connecting an organization's future with its present. These characteristics are:

1. Begins with a desired future state. The user first analyzes the future state, then analyzes the present state of the organization to determine linkage points.

2. Requires vision or strategic future. The tool requires that the organization have a statement of vision or strategic future that is the desired future state. The future state is analyzed for key themes or elements that will be linked with the present state.

3. Analyzes the process backwards. The analysis process begins with the assumption that the future state is achieved and works backward to determine the steps leading toward the present state to connect the two.

4. Reveals a network of choices. As the branch point diagram is developed, it reveals alternatives, constraints, interrelationships, decision points, and priority pathways through which the process can work most efficiently.

5. Network developed through phases. The network is developed through a series of steps or phases that resemble long-range planning goals, objectives, strategies, activities, and assessment. The carry-over to long-range and deployment planning is facilitated.

What Is Its Structure?

The model for the Futuring Tree illustrates linking of the desired or preferred future to an organization's present state in graphic form. The preferred future goal identifies where the organization wants to be in its quality journey. The direction of the network activities that connect with the present state of the organization flows from the future goal toward the present state. The alternative pathways, constraints, and key decision points are reflected in the branch point diagram. See Figure 10-1.

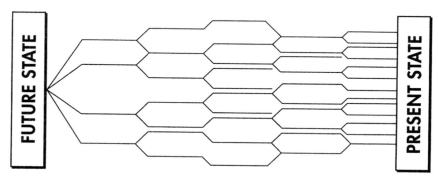

Figure 10-1. The Futuring Tree model.

What Are Examples of Its Use?

Applications of the Futuring Tree process, sometimes called the Relevance Tree, can be seen in several areas where an event, problem, goal, or the like is used as the starting point from which planning is initiated. As an example, environmentalists have pieced together a vision of the earth as a holistic ecological system that is becoming seriously damaged through our careless use of resources and rapid development of technology that causes changes in the ecological balance. The gradual but persistent changes detected in air quality, river and ocean pollution, forests and oil resources, the world's rain forests, the ozone layer, and earth temperatures are signals that help shape a future outcome (vision) which is highly undesirable.

The converse, a positive vision of a restored and ecologically balanced system, has also been offered. Plans for achieving that vision follow the Futuring Tree process of considering where we want to be and reasoning backward from that point through the incremental steps that link us to the present.

A classic example of the Futuring Tree process is the development of Project Apollo by the National Aeronautics and Space Administration (NASA) in the early 1960s. Landing astronauts on the moon, gathering research data, and returning them to earth safely was part of a future space vision accepted and supported by the United States government.

Planning for Project Apollo began with a series of lunar probes collecting valuable data on the nature of the moon. Aside from the myths and mysteries of the moon, scientific information such as measurements of mass, geomagnetic fields, atmospheric quality, timing of its rotation and orbit, surface mapping, preferred landing sites, and capability of life support had to be obtained. Collection and processing of this information strengthened the clarity of the "future state" identified in the tool.

Descending order of planning focused on the Saturn and centaur rockets for propulsion, design of the command module, the lunar excursion module (LEM), and other technology necessary for the project. Decisions on ascent had to be made, which required information gained from the earlier activities. The proposed direct ascent, earth orbiting rendezvous, and the lunar orbiting rendezvous had to be matched with the technical capabilities readily available.

The ensuing funding, training, and communications systems followed, which linked the project to our "present state."

History confirms that Project Apollo met its goals in a safe and successful manner. The success must be attributed to the careful delineation of what the future state is really like and those critical and sequential steps necessary to link the future with the present.

What Is Its Process?

The following steps explain the process of the Futuring Tree. This process follows the initial development of the organization's vision or strategic future.

Futuring Tree

Step 1:   Establish an Appropriate Cross-Functional Team

Step 2:   Develop Key Vision Themes

Step 3:   Define the Present State

Step 4:   Begin the Branch Point Network

Step 5:   Analyze Theme One

Step 6:   Analyze Themes Two, Three, and Four

Step 7:   Form the Completed Network

Step 8:   Identify Priority Pathways

Step 9:   Develop an Action Plan

Figure 10-2. Steps in developing a Futuring Tree.

Step 1: Establish an Appropriate Cross-Functional Team

The first consideration in using the tool is to establish an appropriate cross-functional team of individuals who represent key units in the organization expected to contribute to and support the development of a vision or description of the desired future state of the organization five to ten years from now. This may be a vision statement, an all-encompassing strategic goal statement, or other end goal related to the organization's future. If the organization has a current vision statement, this may be used as the future goal. If not, the process will go on hold until a statement is developed and agreed upon through member consensus. Once the statement is developed it becomes the starting point for the tool. A modified vision statement taken from a state college is presented as an example of a future goal and to show how the analysis is conducted.

Sample Vision Statement

The College of New Jersey anticipates and exceeds the needs of society and the workplace by providing the highest quality educational experiences for its students and employees, supported by excellent research and service. This is accomplished in a community of learners environment where beliefs are translated into actions.

We believe that:

1. Service to the people of the state and the nation is the college's highest priority and should be increased. We serve by preparing our students to be tomorrow's leaders.

2. The college is committed to excellence, embracing those programs and activities that we can deliver at an exemplary level.

3. The college is enriched by the diversity of its people. Diversity gives meaning to sense of community. It enhances creativity, teaches flexibility, and builds strength from difference.

4. A community of learners is built around high expectations. We expect all members to use their unique talents to make the college a better place to learn.

5. We live our ideals within boundaries that heighten our commitment to service, excellence, diversity, and community. We define the college as primarily undergraduate but offering both undergraduate and graduate degrees, giving primacy to teaching, having an achievement-oriented and diverse student body, in a medium-sized, residential, and comprehensive liberal arts institution.*

---

* Adapted from The College of New Jersey Vision Statement.

Step 2: Develop Key Vision Themes

Though vision statements vary in length from a simple phrase to several paragraphs, they all tend to be comprehensive in their intent. Because of this, it is necessary to analyze the statement for its critical themes. When separated out and listed succinctly, these themes form criteria guidelines for success, particularly when faced with constraints and critical decisions during the analysis process. An example of succinct themes of the vision statement follows:

- Expanding service to the people of the state and nation is the college's highest priority.

- The college is committed to excellence, embracing those programs and activities that can be delivered at an exemplary level.

- The college is enriched by the diversity of its students and employees.

- The community of learners is built around high expectations; all members are expected to utilize their unique talents to make the college a better place to learn.

As in any decision-making process, there should be criteria to guide the process. These criteria may be derived from the vision themes listed previously. These key themes are further analyzed to ascertain their salient points. Summaries of each of these should be reviewed by the team and positioned as parameters to be used when approaching alternative pathways and critical decisions in the network of activities. A sample of condensed criteria guidelines is shown below.

Sample Criteria Guidelines: An analysis of the vision statement themes above suggests that the college is committed to:

> *Expanding service to the state and nation*
> *Consistent academic excellence*
> *Enrichment through diversity*
> *Fostering a community of learners*

Step 3: Define the Present State

The team must now look at where the organization is presently. It is recommended that a similar analysis be made to identify those elements that accurately describe the current status of the organization relative to the future goal. This analysis may be extracted from the mission statement or a general description of purpose taken from the organizational profile in an accreditation assessment report, such as the Middlestates report. When these elements are identified, it will be possible to determine the gap that exists between where the organization is and where it wants to be. A network of alternative pathways may then be engineered to bridge the gap and connect the future goal with the present state. A sample description of the present state follows.

Description of Present State

The college is in the process of improving the academic excellence of its students by being more selective in admissions and placement of students. The college has restructured its liberal arts core requirements to build a foundation of higher standards and broader options for students in all majors. A strong academic advisement program has been developed to provide guidance to students, in order to increase retention rates and academic success. Graduate and undergraduate programs are continuously reviewed for state-of-the-art quality. The college has a student minority enrollment of approximately 18 percent and a faculty-staff minority composition of 22 percent. New programs to attract minorities are being developed to align with the population demographics across the state. Classes are now scheduled from early Monday morning through Friday afternoons, with an increasing number of social activities being provided during weekends to entice students to remain on campus. This is done to increase the number of resident students, thereby enhancing the community of learners concept.

Step 4: Begin the Branch Point Network

To begin developing the branch point network, it is important to review the analysis procedure. As described earlier, analysis may be operationally defined as *reasoning backward*. The well-known fictitious detective Sherlock Holmes is a master at this. Holmes is typically faced with a crime and must reason backward to discover the activities and events that led up to the crime. He must create a network of possible events and activities as he gathers and analyzes information. Once this network is developed, his task is to find those common threads winding through the network which connect the criminal with the victim. Variables such as motive, alibi, suspect, conditions at the crime scene, and the like are used as guidelines at the decision-making points encountered along the network.

The Futuring Tree addresses a fundamental inquiry, namely, what decisions, activities, and events must take place in order to connect the future goal with the organization's present state. The team initiates the analysis by asking the following question: *What decisions, activities, and/or events must occur in order for this to be the next logical step?* The question is repeated for each answer, similar to the "5-why" technique for finding root cause. This is done until an answer is obtained that coincides with all or a portion of the description of the organization's present state. Once the analysis reaches this point, a "docking" or connecting procedure is exercised to link the two positions.

Step 5: Analyze Theme One

The team must analyze the key vision themes for the direction each represents. In this example, four themes are identified. The team may divide into four subgroups with each responsible for one of the themes, or it may choose to analyze all four as a team. It is recommended that one theme be analyzed at a time for better thoroughness. See Figure 10-3.

Team members begin the analysis by posting the first theme, *Increased service to the state and nation,* on a section of butcher's paper attached to a wall or on a flip chart. The team then considers the analysis question: *What decisions, activities, and/or events must occur in order for this to be the next logical step?* Team members respond by writing proposed answers on Post-its and posting them vertically to the right of the theme statement, as shown in Figure 10-4. Each proposed answer is reviewed critically and accepted or deferred by the team. This may be done by multi-vote or the nominal group technique if consensus is not reached on the first cut of answers. Two options were selected, which are placed in the branch point diagram as shown in Figure 10-5.

Phase Two is now addressed by brainstorming a vertical list of answers to the analysis question for both responses shown in Figure 10-5. The selection procedure is repeated until Phase Two is complete. See Figure 10-6.

The analysis may be facilitated by viewing the steps in the process as *phases.* The brainstorming and selection of the two statements in Figure

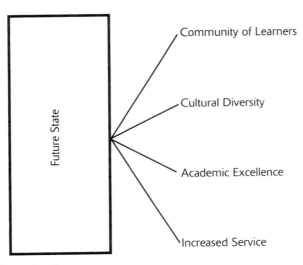

Figure 10-3. Key vision themes.

10-5 represent one phase, which is basically a goal setting phase. In this example, two goals have been established that will drive the remainder of the analysis. This is called Phase One. The analysis process may require as few as five and as many as seven phases, depending upon the nature of the organization and the size of the gap. For purposes of the example provided in this chapter, six phases are needed to bridge the gap between the future goal and the organization's present state. An overview of these phases is shown in

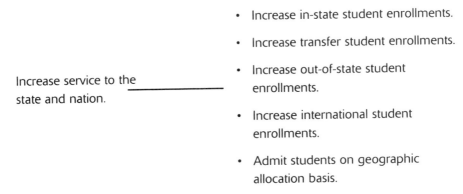

Figure 10-4. Brainstorming responses for Phase One.

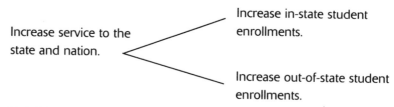

Figure 10-5. Selected responses to Phase One.

Figure 10-7. Using the concept of phases will assist teams in understanding the kinds of things that come next in the analysis.

It is interesting to note that the sequence of phases tends to parallel the strategic and long-range planning processes, with emphasis on deployment. The theme is listed as the *major initiative* for action. Phase One identifies what might be called the *goals*. Phase two produces *objective level statements*, which are a breakdown of the goals. Phase Three describes basic *strategies*, followed by *actions* in Phase Four. Phases Five and Six focus on *data collection* and *obtaining approvals* as well as support for undertaking the journey toward the future goal. In this example, the connections with the present state are made in Phase Six. A completed sample analysis for Theme One is provided in Figure 10-8. Note the emerging decision points and opportunities the college must consider in developing a pathway connecting its future goal with the present state.

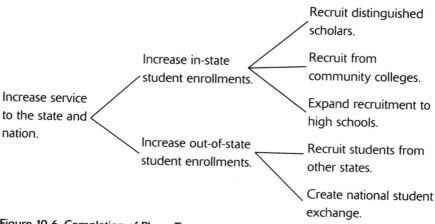

Figure 10-6. Completion of Phase Two.

Phase Description

Phase 1	Phase 2	Phase 3	Phase 4	Phase 5	Phase 6
Identification of Desired Change Categories	Identification of Specific Changes	Identification of Focused Strategies	Identification of Activities that Bring Changes	Collection and Analysis of Information	Obtainment of Approval and Support
Statements in Phase 1 describe key changes desired to bring the organization to its future state. These changes represent clusters of smaller changes that are identified in Phase 2. Statements in Phase 1 are similar to organization goals.	Statements in Phase 2 describe specific changes desired that constitute the goals identified in Phase 1. Phase 2 statements are similar to *objectives* in their focus.	Statements in Phase 3 explain how the specific changes are accomplished. They list focused *strategies* that are proposed to reach Phase 2.	Statements in Phase 4 list *activities* that combine with Phase 3 strategies to achieve the desired changes. The activities selected are key to the successful change process.	Statements in Phase 5 describe what *information* and *data* needs to be collected, and how it will be analyzed to contribute to the change process.	Statements in Phase 6 identify those areas that require *approval* and *support* of the organization. Areas not listed have authority to initiate change toward the future state.

Figure 10-7. Descriptions of the phases.

Step 6: Analyze Themes Two, Three, and Four

The second theme should be selected and analyzed. If the whole team plans to analyze all four themes, it is helpful to select a theme that may have some interface with the first one. For example, if Theme Two, *Increase cultural diversity of students, faculty, and staff*, were analyzed next, there may be a natural interface with Theme One at Phase Two; that is, the two responses, *Recruit minority faculty and staff* and *Increase minority student recruitment*, will interface with *Create a national student exchange* in Theme One. The interfacing will become more obvious as the analyses are superimposed on one generic network. If, however, the themes are analyzed separately, an attempt can be made, when complete, to align the two themes if and where they may interface. This analysis is continued for Themes Three and Four. The advantage of using Post-its is to allow flexibility in aligning the four themes when they are merged into one master diagram later on.

Step 7: Form the Completed Network

Once all four themes are completed, they are assembled into a master branch point diagram that displays the network of pathways, decisions, constraints, and options available for connecting the present state with the organization's future goal. A closer review of the network will assist the user in identifying those pathways that can expedite the linking process.

Step 8: Identify Priority Pathways

When the connection is made, the team should backtrack through the network to identify those pathways that the organization can follow to reach its future goal most efficiently. This may be accomplished on a theme-by-theme basis or by identifying pathways throughout the integrated network that will cut across themes. The pathways may vary from organization to organization depending upon the leadership and resources. Some may choose the easiest pathways, making it much easier to navigate the network, whereas other organizations may choose the more challenging paths. Priority pathways will be established based upon the organization's needs and resources.

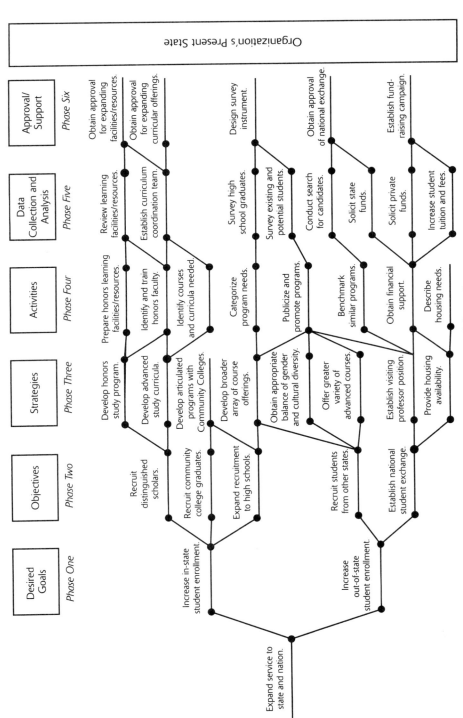

Figure 10-8. Sample analysis of Theme One—increase service to the state and the nation.

Step 9: Develop an Action Plan

The next logical step is to develop an action plan to guide the organization through the network to the future goal. The action plan should be based on the priority pathways that identify the directions the plan will follow. Things to consider in the action plan are:

1. What needs to be done to reach the goal?

2. Who will be responsible for each task?

3. How much time is required to accomplish the action plan?

4. Are the appropriate human resources available within the organization to complete the required tasks?

5. Are there sufficient financial resources available to pursue the action plan?

6. Are the physical facilities and available technology capable of supporting the plan?

7. How will progress on the action plan be assessed?

The Action Plan Matrix shown in Figure 10-9 provides a means of deriving answers to these questions. The process may also be flowcharted for greater detail.

The information provided by the Futuring Tree is guided by criteria established early by the project team. These criteria strengthen the systematic nature of the procedure and prevent the analysis from straying outside of set parameters.

Future projections are often stated in very brief form, sometimes as short as a single paragraph consisting of three or four sentences. It is also not uncommon to find vision statements so brief that they become slogans that can have several interpretations. Examples of these are, "Quality is job number one at . . . ," "You're in good hands with . . . ," and "Be all you can be."

The Futuring Tree requires that the vision or future goal be carefully thought through and expressed so that key themes may be identified to guide the analysis process that links the goal with the present state. It is difficult, after having established a future goal, to find efficient pathways to that goal by beginning where the organization is and reaching into the future without the benefit of predisposed direction. As the Apollo Project engineers at NASA

Action Tasks	Person Responsible	Time Required for Completion	Amount/Source of Funds	Appropriate Personnel	Technology and Facilities	Means of Assessment
1.						
2.						
3.						
4.						
5.						
6.						
7.						
8.						
9.						
10.						
11.						
12.						

Figure 10-9. Action plan matrix.

discovered, it made more sense to begin their analysis with an imaginary person who has landed on the moon and think backward through the many steps that had to be accomplished before the Apollo Project could become a reality. This process of reasoning backward was used by NASA and proved to be very successful.

This tool is most effective when an organization forecasts into the intermediate or long-range future, when the likelihood of future situations and events happening is clear.

What Are Variations of this Tool?

The simplest variation is to use the standard Tree Diagram from the management and planning tools published by GOAL/QPC. The Tree Diagram and branch point network use the same procedure to analyze the tasks required to reach an end goal. See Figure 10-10.

Other variations include the Activity Network Diagram (also from GOAL/QPC) and the Program Evaluation and Review Technique (PERT). Each of these procedures generates a series of sequential activities and events that connect two end variables. This type of procedure tends to be very task-oriented during the analysis procedure and reduces the number of options that might be available to the organization. See Figures 10-11 and 10-12.

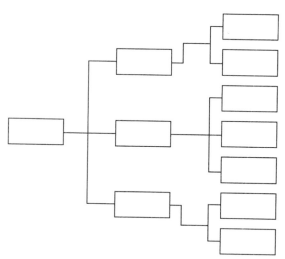

Figure 10-10. Sample Tree Diagram.

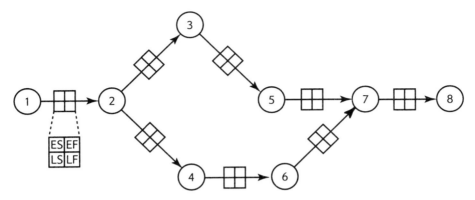

Figure 10-11. Sample Activity Network (arrow) diagram with boxes for showing earliest start (ES) and finish (EF) times as well as latest start (LS) and finish (LF) times. Courtesy of GOAL/QPC.

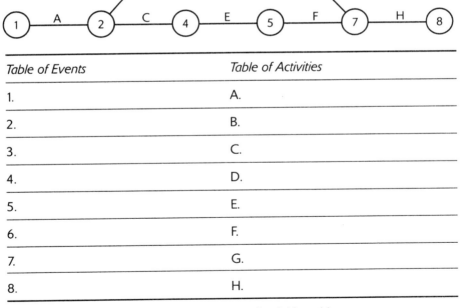

Table of Events	Table of Activities
1.	A.
2.	B.
3.	C.
4.	D.
5.	E.
6.	F.
7.	G.
8.	H.

Figure 10-12. Sample PERT chart with events and activities tables.

References

Brassard, M. 1989. *The Memory Jogger Plus +*. Methuen, MA: GOAL/QPC, p. 71–96, p. 197–229.

Caidin, M. 1963. *The Moon: New World for Men*. New York: Bobbs-Merrill Company.

Cornesky, R., ed. June 1993. "TQM Tools and Techniques." *TQM in Higher Education*. Madison, WI: Magna Publications. vol. 2, no. 6, 4–5.

Kurtzman, J. 1984. *Futurcasting*. Palm Springs, CA: ETC Publications.

Scholtes, P. 1992. *The Team Handbook*. Madison, WI: Joiner Associates, 2–18 to 2–24.

Tribus, M. 1989. *Deployment Flow Charting*. Los Angeles: Quality and Productivity.

Walton, M. 1986. *The Deming Management Method*. New York: Putnam Publishing Group.

Select Bibliography

"Analysis of Delphi Technique Survey." 1991. Cherry Hill Public Schools.

Armstrong, J. S. 1985. *Long-Range Forecasting: From Crystal Ball to Computer*. 2d ed. New York: John Wiley & Sons (Exhibit 14-1).

Barker, J. A. 1985. *Discovering the Future: The Business of Paradigms*. St. Paul, MN: ILI Press.

———. 1992. *Future Edge*. New York: William Morrow and Company, p. 21.

———. 1994. *Implications Wheel*. A video by Aurora Pictures in Minneapolis, MN 55406-9861.

Bauman, P. 1996. *Governing Education: Public Sector Reform or Privatization*. Needham Heights, MA: Allyn & Bacon.

Brassard, M. 1988. *The Memory Jogger*. Methuen, MA: GOAL/QPC.

———. 1989. *The Memory Jogger Plus*. Methuen, MA: GOAL/QPC.

———. 1989. *The Memory Jogger Plus +*. Methuen, MA: GOAL/QPC, p. 71–96, 197–229.

———. 1988. *The Memory Jogger Plus + Featuring the Seven Management and Planning Tools*. Methuen, MA: GOAL/QPC.

———. 1995. *The Memory Jogger II*. Methuen, MA: GOAL/QPC.

Brassard, M., and D. Ritter. 1994. *The Memory Jogger II*. Methuen, MA: GOAL/QPC.

Caidin, M. 1963. *The Moon: New World for Men*. New York: Bobbs-Merrill Company.

Capon, N., and J. M. Hulbert. 1987. "Forecasting and Strategic Planning." *The Handbook of Forecasting*. New York: John Wiley & Sons, p. 75–79.

Caravatta, M. 1997. *Let's Work Smarter, Not Harder.* American Society for Quality, Milwaukee, WI: Quality Press.

Cetron, M., and M. Gayle. 1991. *Educational Renaissance: Our Schools at the Turn of the 21st Century.* New York: St. Martins Press.

Chandler, R. 1992. *Racing Towards 2001: The Forces Shaping America's Religious Future.* Grand Rapids, MI: Zondervan Publishing House.

Cherry Hill Public Schools. February 1995. *Report of the Cherry Hill Public Schools' Strategic Planning Committee.* Cherry Hill, NJ: p. 2.

Collett, C. et al. 1992. *Making Daily Management Work.* Methuen, MA: GOAL/QPC.

Cook, W. J. Jr. 1990. *Strategic Planning.* Washington, D.C.: American Association of School Administrators, p. 5, 71–75.

Corestates Bank of Delaware. Undated. *Core Values.* Wilmington, DE: The Corestates Bank.

Cornesky, R., ed. June 1993. "TQM Tools and Techniques." *TQM in Higher Education.* Madison, WI: Magna Publications. vol. 2, no. 6, p. 4–5.

Cowley, M., and E. Domb. 1997. *Beyond Strategic Vision.* Methuen, MA: GOAL/QPC.

Crawford, C., J. Demidovich, and R. Krone. July 1984. *Productivity Improvement by the Crawford Slip Method.* Los Angeles: University of Southern California School of Public Administration.

Cunningham, W,. and D. Gresso. 1994. *Cultural Leadership: The Culture of Excellence in Education.* Needham Heights, MA: Allyn & Bacon.

Dakley, N., and O. Helmer. 1963. "An Experimental Approach of the Delphi Method to the Use of Experts." *Management Science,* vol. 9, no. 3, p. 458.

Demidovich, J. M. January 1983. *Crawford Slip Method: Brainpower by Think Tank Technology.* Los Angeles: University of Southern California School of Public Administration.

Deming, W. E. 1986. *Out Of The Crisis.* Cambridge, MA: Massachusetts Institute of Technology, p. 23.

———. 1993. *The New Economy.* Cambridge, MA: Massachusetts Institute of Technology Center for Advanced Engineering Study, p. 104–5.

Dettmer, J., R. Krone, and J. Gould. 1989. *Brainpower Networking in Support of TQM Implementation.* A paper presented at the first National Total Quality Management Symposium in Denver, Colorado, November 3.

Fildes, R. 1987. "Forecasting: The Issues," *The Handbook of Forecasting: A Manager's Guide.* New York: John Wiley & Sons, p. 161

Fowles, J. 1978. *Handbook of Futures Research.* Westport, CT: Greenwood Press.

Global Business Network and the National Education Associations Scenario Project. 1994. Internet: www.GBN.ORG/SCENARIOS/NEA/NEA.HTML

Goodstein, L. P., T. Nolan, and J. W. Pfiffer. 1993. *Applied Strategic Planning*. New York: McGraw Hill, p. 3.

Hack, W., C. Candoli, and J. Roy. 1995. School Business Administration. 5th ed. Needham Heights, MA: Allyn & Bacon.

Hamel, G., and C. K. Prahalad. 1994. *Competing for the Future*. Boston, MA: Harvard Business School Press, ix, 82.

Hammer, M., and J. Champy. 1993. *Reengineering the Corporation*. New York: Harper Collins, p. 32.

Hanson, E. M. 1996. *Educational Administration and Organizational Behavior*. 4th ed. Needham Heights, MA: Allyn & Bacon.

Hax, A., and N. Majluf. 1991. *The Strategy Process and Concept—A Pragmatic Approach*. Englewood Cliffs, NJ: Prentice-Hall.

Helmer, O. 1987. "Problems in Futures Research—Delphi and Causal Cross-Impact Analysis." *Futures*. vol. 9, p.71.

Hencley, S. P., and J. R. Yates. 1974. *Futurism in Education*. Berkeley, CA: McCutchen Publishing Corporation, p. 12–26, 115–126.

Hesselbein, F., M. Goldsmith, and R. Beckhard. 1996. *The Leader of the Future*. New York: The Drucker Foundation.

Hoffherr, G. D. 1993. *The Toolbook: Decision Making & Planning for Optimum Results*. Windham, NH: Markon.

Ignatovich, F. R. 1974. "Morphological Analysis." Chapter 10 in *Futurism In Education* by Henclay and Yates. Berkeley, CA: McCutcheon Publishing Corporation, p. 211–233.

Imai, M. 1986. *KAIZEN*. New York: Random House Business Division, p. 3, 25.

Jones, H., and B. C. Twiss. 1978. *Forecasting Technology for Planning Decisions*. New York: Petrocelli Books.

Joseph, E. C. 1974. "An Introduction to Studying the Future." *Futurism in Education*. Berkeley, CA: McCutchen Publishing Corporation, p. 2–3.

Kahn, H., and A. J. Weiner. 1967. *The Year 2000: A Framework for Speculation on the Next Thirty-Three Years*. New York: Macmillan.

Kendall, G. 1998. *Securing the Future: Strategies for Exponential Growth Using the Theory of Constraints*. Boca Raton, FL: St. Lucie Press.

King, B. 1989. *Hoshin Planning: The Developmental Approach*. Methuen, MA: GOAL/QPC.

Kurtzman, J. 1984. *Futurcasting*. Palm Springs, CA: ETC Publications.

Levelback, H., and J. P. Cleary. 1981. *The Beginning Forecaster: The Forecasting Process through Data Analysis*. Belmont, CA: Lifetime Learning Publications, p. 3.

Makridakis, S. 1990. *Forecasting, Planning, and Strategy for the 21st Century*. New York: The Free Press.

Makridakis, S., and S. C. Wheelwright. 1979. "Forecasting: Framework and Overview." *Forecasting*. Ed., S. Makridakis and S. C. Wheelwright. TIMS Studies in the Management Series, vol. 12, North-Holland, Amsterdam.

————. 1987. *The Handbook of Forecasting: A Manager's Guide*. New York: John Wiley & Sons, p. 12–14.

Malcolm Baldrige National Quality Award Criteria for Performance Excellence, 1998. Gaithersburg, MD: National Institute of Standards and Technology.

Malcolm Baldrige National Quality Award Criteria for Performance Excellence in Education, 1998. Gaithersburg, MD: National Institute of Standards and Technology.

Marrus, S. 1984. *Building the Strategic Plan*. New York: John Wiley & Sons, p. 4.

Martino, J. 1983. *Technological Forecasting for Decision Making*. 2d ed. New York: North Holland Publishers, p. 78.

MBNQA. 1995. *Midstate University Case Study*. Gaithersburg, MD: National Institute of Standards and Technology, p. 1.

Millett, S. M., and E. J. Honton. 1991. *A Manager's Guide to Technology Forecasting and Strategy Analysis Methods*. Columbus, OH: Battle Press, p. 2.

Millett, S. M., and E. J. Honton. 1991. *A Manager's Guide to Technology Forecasting and Statistical Analysis Methods*. Columbus: Battle Press.

Naisbitt, J., and P. Aberdene. 1990. *Megatrends 2000*. New York: William Morrow and Company.

Nanus, B. 1992. *Visionary Leadership*. San Francisco: Jossey-Bass Publishers, p. 8.

Norris, D.. and N. Poulton. 1991. *A Guide for New Planners*. Ann Arbor, MI: The Society for College and University Planning, p. 9–11.

Norton, M. S., L. D. Webb, L. Dlugash, and W. Sybouts. 1996. *The School Superintendency: New Responsibilities, New Leadership*. Needham Heights, MA: Allyn & Bacon.

Owens, R. 1994. *Organizational Behavior in Education*. 5th ed. Needham Heights, MA: Allyn & Bacon.

Ozeki, K., and T. Asaka. 1990. *Handbook of Quality Tools: The Japanese Approach*. Cambridge: Productivity Press.

Rothwell, W,. and H. C. Kazanas. 1994. *Planning and Managing Human Resources*. Amherst, MA: HRD Press, p. 1–2.

Scherkenbach, W. 1990. *The Deming Route to Quality and Productivity*. Rockville, MD: Mercury Press, p. 13.

————. 1991. *Deming's Road to Continual Improvement*. Knoxville: SPC Press, p. 196.

Schoemaker, P. J. H. 1995. "Scenario Planning: A Tool for Strategic Thinking." *Sloan Management Review* (winter).

Scholtes, P. 1992. *The Team Handbook*. Madison, WI: Joiner Associates, p. 2–18 to 2–24.

Schwartz, P. 1995. *The Art of the Long View*. New York: Doubleday Currency.

Senge, P. 1990. *The Fifth Discipline*. New York: Currency and Doubleday Publishers, p. 12.

Sergiovanni, T. 1995. *The Principalship: A Reflective Practice Perspective*. 3rd ed. Needham Heights, MA: Allyn & Bacon.

Shipley, J. 1993. *Total Quality Schooling: A Plan to Empower a Community*. Largo, FL: Pinellas County School District, The Quality Academy.

Sullivan, W. G., and W. W. Claycombe. 1977. *Fundamentals of Forecasting*. Reston, VA: Reston Publishing Company, p. 3.

Tribus, M. 1989. *Deployment Flow Charting*. Los Angeles: Quality and Productivity.

Ubben, G. 1997. *The Principalship: Creative Leadership for Effective Schools*. 3rd ed. Needham Heights, MA: Allyn & Bacon.

Uchida, D., M. Cetron, and F. McKenzie. 1996. *Preparing Students for the 21st Century*. Arlington, VA: American Association of School Administrators.

Walton, M. 1986. *The Deming Management Method*. New York: Putnam Publishing Group.

Weisbord, M., and S. Janoff. 1995. *Future Search: An Action Guide to Finding Common Ground in Organizations and Communities*. San Francisco: Berrett-Koehler.

Wheelwright, S. C., and S. Makridakis. 1985. *Forecasting Methods for Management*. New York: John Wiley & Sons, p. 10–19.

Whitley, R. C. 1991. *The Customer-Driven Company: Moving from Talk to Action*. Reading, MA: Addison-Wesley Publishing Company, p. 26.

Zwicky, F. 1969. *Invention, Research, Through the Morphological Approach*. Toronto: MacMillan.

————. 1962. "Morphology of Propulsive Power," *Monographs on Morphological Research*. No. 1. Pasadena, CA: Society for Morphological Research.

Index